RAW FOOD
FRENCH STYLE

delphine de montalier

RAW FOOD
FRENCH STYLE

115 fresh recipes from the
new generation of french chefs

Photography by David Japy

Styling by Elodie Rambaud

Illustrations by Jane Teasdale

Translation by Alexandra Carlier

FRANCES LINCOLN LIMITED
PUBLISHERS

FOREWORD

Some people might say that eating raw is just a trend or the latest fad. But it is so much more than that. Eating raw is a holistic approach to wellbeing: it concerns our health, our body and our planet.

I realize that this book is not going to solve all the challenges of healthy living, least of all the way you approach your diet. I see the book as just a little step in the right direction: it paves the way for a change in your shopping and eating habits, it offers recipes bursting with nutrients and all the goodness that nature so generously provides.

I would not describe myself as an exclusive crudivore or raw foodist. However, I do want to eat healthily, source the best possible products, and rediscover the authentic taste of untreated fruit and vegetables.

Raw food is an inexhaustible response to these basic human desires. Raw food is a celebration of nature: joyful, light hearted, colourful, crunchy and packed with vitamins. It is also quickly prepared.

At the same time raw food demands high standards in the way that it is cultivated. Shopping and sourcing high-quality food does not necessarily mean you have to abandon the supermarket completely and move on exclusively to organic greengrocers and suppliers. It does imply, however, that you should be alert to what is on offer. For those of you who remain sceptical about the benefits of organic food, I extend an invitation to you to change your habits just a little each time you shop. Look at the labels, consider the sources of supply and generally be more aware of what you are buying. Whenever you can, opt for produce that is grown locally and, above all, choose the produce of the season. The message of this book, in terms of producers, is think small.

In my choice of recipes, I have tried to please the greatest number of users. Committed raw foodists will be delighted to find a category of recipes marked 100% raw. Into this category (of uniquely raw food products), I have included some fish because I know that some raw foodists cannot live without it. For food-lovers in general, I have devised raw recipes with a twist which is not really 'raw' at all. In these recipes you will find cheese, cream and even chorizo sausage. For meat-eaters, there is everything you need to get your full ration of protein. And following the spirit if not the letter of Raw Food, there are recipes in the Barely Cooked chapter which are cooked very quickly. You will also find soups which lend themselves to being heated, and thereby cooked.

I am also providing you with some surprise guests: contributions from an exciting new generation of chefs and restaurateurs with a real talent for raw food. I thank them for having so kindly given me a special recipe for this book.

Delphine

CONTENTS

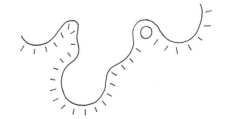

USER'S GUIDE

THE RAW PANTRY

One thing is certain: I am not suggesting that you rush out immediately to your favourite health-food store to stock up on all of these ingredients!

SPICES

black pepper
Cayenne pepper
cinnamon
cumin
Espelette pepper
ginger
nutmeg
Sichuan (Szechuan) pepper

――

DRIED FRUIT

dates
figs
raisins

――

SWEETENERS

agave syrup (nectar)
maple syrup
organic whole cane sugar (radapura)
soft light brown sugar (raw caster)
soft dark brown sugar
unpasteurised honey

――

MILKS

almond milk
coconut milk
coconut water
hazelnut milk
soy milk

――

NUTS & SEEDS

almonds
black sesame seeds
caraway seeds
cashew nuts
chia seeds
fennel seeds
hazelnuts
hemp seeds
linseeds (flaxseeds)
macadamia nuts
mustard seeds
nigella seeds
peanuts
pine nuts
pistachio nuts
poppy seeds
pumpkin seeds (pepitas)
sesame seeds
sunflower seeds

――

The following list is intended as an indication of the basic dry-store ingredients associated with the preparation of raw food recipes. You can build up your pantry gradually, choosing items as your mood and taste buds take you and, above all, depending on the recipes you want to make. I have also set the most 'indispensable' products in bold, indicating those that are used most often in my recipes.

SEASONINGS

fleur de sel
gomasio
Himalayan salt
nuoc cham sauce (fish sauce)
organic soy sauce
sea salt
tamari sauce
white miso

— —

PURÉES & NUT BUTTERS

almond purée (butter)
cashew nut purée (butter)
coconut butter
hazelnut purée (butter)
Tahini (sesame purée)

— —

OILS & VINEGARS

apple cider vinegar
cold-pressed extra virgin olive oil
'cream' of balsamic vinegar, a syrupy reduction
grape seed oil
hazelnut oil
pumpkin seed oil
rapeseed oil (canola oil)
rice vinegar
sesame oil
sunflower oil
umeboshi (Japanese plum) vinegar
wine vinegar

— —

MISCELLANEOUS INGREDIENTS

capers
carob or cocoa powder
dried bonito flakes
edible seaweed: dulse seaweed, nori sheets and
wakame sheets
lemon confit
oyster leaves
shiso leaves
soy lecithin
sun-dried tomatoes
Tabasco sauce
vanilla pods (beans)
wakame sheets
wasabi

— —

USER'S GUIDE

EQUIPMENT

Simply reading this book will not make you want to upgrade your kitchen equipment; to rush out and buy the latest piece of kit, like a tempting new food processor with seemingly endless functions or a fancy masticating juicer, or even a solar oven or dehydrator. This is not the message I am sending to my readers. In any case, it would not be worth it: unless you are going to devote yourself from this moment on to an entirely raw diet, you will be able to manage perfectly well, for the most part, with the equipment you already own. Having said that, raw food often has a firmer or crunchier texture than its cooked equivalent and this sometimes affects the type of kitchen equipment you use. A further consideration is that raw food is associated with the preservation of nutrients, which are often damaged by violent mechanical motion and the build-up of heat in a machine. Therefore, the guidelines which follow should help you to enjoy and reap to the fullest extent the beneficial vitamins and minerals that raw food recipes contain.

ELECTRICAL APPLIANCES

THE FOOD PROCESSOR

Nowadays, food processors vary enormously in their power and ever-increasing range of functions. We probably all have one of these in the kitchen with varying degrees of options and attachments, including interchangeable rotary blades. Even a basic model should not be underestimated. It will probably have a wide roomy bowl and its blades and discs will slice, chop, grate, mix and whisk, and so help you make many of the recipes in this book. Often these machines are referred to as 'robot chefs' or 'robots' or even Magimix. Modern versions have a blendermix attachment which will blend and liquidize soft ingredients. In order to purée solid and semi-solid food, such as raw hard fruits and vegetables, a powerful, multi-purpose version is required. At the top end of the high performance range, Vitamix is a well-established brand which specializes in its blending functions and so calls itself a versatile blender rather than a food processor. Versatile in the extreme, the Vitamix combines ten appliances, including a sorbetière, a grinder and a centrifugal juicer. I'm fortunate enough to have something similar, notably a Thermomix, which not only boasts inbuilt scales and a heating element, but also works as a very effective tool for performing all the tasks required for the recipes in this book. One advantage of the more sophisticated models is that they allow you to control the speed, and therefore limit the build up of heat in the machine, very easily.

THE REGULAR BLENDER

This usually has a tall vertical bowl and is sometimes referred to as a liquidizer. It will blend to a purée a range of ingredients with a soft texture - for example, bananas, berry fruits or avocados. Such ingredients might be combined with a liquid element. With its emphasis on soft ingredients, this type of blender is often used for puréeing vegetables which have been softened by cooking. Whether cooked or raw, the purée is the stepping stone to further preparations, such as sauces and soups. If, once you have achieved the purée, the texture seems too thick or grainy for your needs, you can pass the mixture though a nylon sieve before puréeing it again. When it comes to breaking down and blending raw hard fruits and vegetables to a purée, then cheaper models will not be capable of the task, particularly if there is very little liquid added to the bowl.

IMMERSION BLENDER

While food processors and regular blenders require the food to be placed in the machine's special bowl, the immersion blender – also called a stick blender – is very different. It is a wand that is put directly into the food, regardless of what type of bowl or pan it is in. There are cordless and corded versions. These liberating tools come with several different blade attachments which can pulverize soft and semi-firm food items to a purée, and can also whisk and froth.

——

THE CHOPPER

Once upon a time the chopper was an inbuilt function of a food-processor. Now, however, the chopper has reinvented itself as an independent compact tool with a small bowl which sits neatly on the work counter. Some are so compact they are rightly called 'mini' choppers. Bigger versions are usually multi-functional and make even-shaped dice. They all make light work of chopping. Superior models also have an emulsifying blade which is good for making mayonnaise or vinaigrettes.

——

THE CENTRIFUGAL JUICER

This is a good tool for most juices, especially those extracted from firm raw vegetables and hard fruits. For a relatively small outlay you have the means to make, say, carrot and apple juice very quickly and efficiently. However, the centrifugal type of juicer employs a high-speed spinning action. Moreover, within its spinning chamber, teeth shred the ingredients to a pulp and this action raises the temperature of the ingredients and so damages, to some degree, their enzymes and natural health-giving properties. For this reason, you should not make it run fast. But you know that by now!

——

THE MASTICATING JUICER

This machine is a better tool than the centrifugal juicer when it comes to getting all that is good from leafy vegetables and herbs. Here we are really talking about the stuff of raw-food buffs. The machine's key feature is its slow chewing action which resembles the action of human teeth. This neither overheats nor damages the ingredients so that all their natural goodness is preserved – so spinach, sorrel, wheatgrass, parsley, lambsquarters, and so on, come to you in their purest possible form. But the machine is not cheap. Next to opening your own juice bar, buying a masticating juicer for your morning energy boost may seem to some a little over the top. But it is not forbidden to treat yourself to something that is so good for you!

——

NON-ELECTRICAL GADGETS
MULTI-FUNCTIONAL GRATERS AND SPIRAL VEGETABLE SLICERS

There are now so many different types of graters, slicers and spiral cutters available that are so simple to use, they can only entice you to cut cubes, slices, julienne strips and strings from the most firm of fruit and vegetables. The spirelli spiral slicer and cutter (available online) is little more than a metal tube which ideally suits cylindrical shaped vegetables such as carrots, courgettes (zucchini), cucumber and white Daikon radish. To obtain long spaghetti strings, you gently push the item through and twist. That's it! GEFU is a particularly good brand of spirelli spiral slicer. The latest mandolines also have an array of inspiring attachments for making juliennes, tagliatelles and the fanciest of long curls and twists. But, as with any of these tools, watch your fingers. Choose solid, quality tools with sharp blades and good casings. Check that they will be easy to clean. They will last, bring pleasure and, most importantly, make you want to prepare raw food creatively. They are also perfect for those of us who might be venturing into the field of raw food for the first time.

——

USER'S GUIDE

KNIVES AND PEELERS

With just a good old-fashioned, well-sharpened knife and a quality vegetable peeler, you can have a lot of fun with your vegetables. You can not only remove peel but also take thin carpaccio-like slices from your vegetables and fruits. Peelers are also a good way of scraping away shavings of fresh Parmesan. These small tools are my basics! I always have them with me, and I replace them at the slightest sign of wear. A peeler can have a straight handle or a Y-shaped one with a swivel action blade. For slicing and cutting small vegetables, such as pink radish, use a knife with a small blade; conversely a long one for a carrot or parsnip. For slicing meat and fish into paper-thin carpaccio slices, do not hesitate to invest in a first-class knife that you do not have to sharpen every time you use it. Ceramic knives are wonderful because they retain their cutting edge well. But they need to be of a very high quality, so avoid discounted and sale items. Once again, watch out for your fingers when you slice and chop.

– –

ONE CUTTING BOARD OR SEVERAL?

If you often cook with raw meat and fish, then ideally you should have three boards: one for fruit and vegetables, one for meat and another for fish. As to whether they should be made of wood, plastic or glass, it is really a question of taste and daily usage. I love my plastic cutting board because it has a nonporous surface and is easy to put in the dishwasher. However, I also use my wooden board a lot, despite having to scrub it thoroughly after each use, because it is sturdy and does not slip. Mine is made of bamboo but good wooden boards can also be found in beech, sycamore and ash. A little tip: clean boards now and then with a little white vinegar.

– –

FOR DEHYDRATING, STORING, DRYING, ETC.

THE DEHYDRATOR

This makes it possible to dehydrate, and dry, seasonal fruits and vegetables so that you can store them for later. It is an electric appliance that heats and circulates air in a closed container in which you arrange sliced fruit or vegetables on trays. The temperature is, of course, set so that the food retains its nutritional values. Therefore, the hot air enables the water content of the fruit and vegetables to evaporate. You can set the drying time according to several criteria: the ripeness of the food, the size of the pieces and, above all, the final texture you want to achieve – crispy or soft, for instance.

– –

THE OVEN

You don't have a dehydrator at home? Well, neither do I! But I am fortunate enough to have an oven capable of a temperature as low as 40-50°C (100-120°F) in its fan-assisted mode. So, from time to time, I place sliced fruit on several oven racks and wait, patiently, because it takes a very long time! In fact, it takes about the same length of time as a dehydrator, but it uses more electricity and, more importantly perhaps, it monopolizes the oven for hours at a time, which of course is not necessarily a problem for people who only eat raw food!

– –

GLASS JARS AND METAL TINS

The point of drying seasonal fruits is to be able to enjoy them all year round. If the drying process is done properly, the fruit should keep for a year. So, given that you won't be eating the fruit straight away, you will need some quality storage containers. Choose either airtight glass jars or metal tins, and keep them in a dry place away from direct sunlight. One small thing: don't forget to label your containers clearly with the date of storage and a description.

I SPROUT MY OWN SEEDS!

What a pleasure it is to eat seeds you've sown yourself! It reminds me of school, when we would have so much fun growing lentils in cotton… and it worked even then! Germination occurs simultaneously with a biochemical and enzymatic reaction which gives 'nutritional superpowers' to sprouted seeds and seedlings. Basically, vitamins, minerals and essential amino acids are multiplied, providing a concentration of energy. By consuming the sprouts in their raw form, you reap the full benefits of their superpowers!

TYPES OF SEEDS

There is a broad spectrum of seeds available for you to cultivate:
— Grains: oats, wheat, spelt, corn, barley, rice, khorasan wheat (also called Kamut), quinoa, buckwheat…
— Pulses: lentils, white or red kidney beans, chickpeas, green peas, alfalfa (also called lucerne)…
— Oil-bearing seeds: sesame, sunflower, linseed (or flax) almonds, hazelnuts…
— Vegetables and herbs: carrots, celery, fennel, radishes, leeks, rocket, basil…

— —

GLASS-JAR TECHNIQUE

If you are a beginner, then start with a sterilized glass jar and a single type of seed. Rinse and dry the seeds. Put 1-2 tablespoons of seeds in the bottom of the jar then cover the seeds with water. Cover the jar with a piece of muslin or cheesecloth, secured with a rubber band, and let the seeds soak overnight. The next day, drain the seeds and rinse them. Drain them again and make sure they are still slightly moist before returning them to the jar and covering it again with muslin. During the day, repeat this rinsing procedure twice more. Repeat this procedure for 3 days.

— —

SEED-TRAY TECHNIQUE

Start by soaking 2-3 tablespoons of seeds, which is about 10-15 g (^{1}/$_2$–^{3}/$_4$ oz), in spring water. Count one hour for smaller seeds and up to 12 hours for the largest ones. This time-span is what we call the 'wake-up' period. Next, place the seeds on the growing trays and stack them. Precisely how you stack will depend on the type of seed tray you have, so refer to manufacturer's instructions. Put the lid in place and sprinkle with tap water twice daily. Be sure to empty the water collection basin from time to time and to keep the growing trays away from direct sunlight. The seeds will be ready to eat as soon as small white sprouts appear. In order to obtain longer green seedlings, simply prolong the germination process by exposing the seed tray to sunlight for 2-3 extra days. Continue to sprinkle the sprouts with water carefully and regularly in order to keep them moist. One more important piece of advice: rinse your sprouts thoroughly before eating them.

— —

USER'S GUIDE

VEGETABLES: WHERE, WHEN, HOW?

Raw vegetables abound in vitamins, minerals and antioxidants. However, we must guard the nutrients with care and remember that when we heat these nutrients above 43°C (110°F) we damage or destroy them. The best way to reap vegetables' nutritional benefits is to consume them in the form of a raw juice, soup or a smoothie. When you make these preparations using electrical equipment, you should always use the appropriate appliance and take care not to overheat and ruin the ingredients (see page 10). Below you will find my advice about making the most of your consumption of raw vegetables and adopting the right approach to shopping, buying and storing:

GOOD AND ORGANIC

If you only remember one thing about choosing vegetables, it should be quality: if the cost of first-class quality is an issue, then remember that it is better to eat a few excellent specimens than lots of inferior ones – otherwise you might as well eat vegetables from a can! Nowadays, you can find quality vegetables quite easily, whether organically grown or locally grown by responsible farmers. You'll find good vegetables that are organic or produced in responsible farming. It is up to you to sift through your local suppliers, perhaps using internet sites to help, and find a farmer's market or local farm supplier or health-food store that will meet your needs. This is a controversial new trend in shopping behaviour but the vegetables you find in this way do contain fewer chemicals than those sourced through more traditional forms of shopping. One important piece of advice: if, for whatever reason, organic vegetables are not an option for you, then I suggest that you vigorously scrub, wash or peel your vegetables. Because such cautious measures as peeling and scrubbing are not necessary with organic vegetables, it means you can benefit from many vital elements contained in their skin.

– –

ALL RAW, ALL FRESH

Choose the freshest possible vegetables: it is alright if they look a bit weird; it is fine if they have a bizarre shape; it does not matter if they are covered in soil, but they should definitely not look past their best, with wrinkled skin, blemishes or spots.

Buy only seasonal vegetables and local ones if possible. This may be self-evident, but it is nevertheless important to emphasize. Vegetables straight out of the ground are your best choice as well as your eco-friendly contribution to the planet!

Do not buy vegetables in bulk: they go bad quickly. Keep them in the vegetable drawer of your refrigerator or in a cool place away from direct sunlight.

Do not prepare them too far in advance of eating, and eat what you have prepared quickly. Drink fresh vegetable juice immediately. And, above all, chew… again and again!

– –

WHAT A PRO NEEDS

Make sure that you have the right equipment (see page 10) so that you can do lots of different things with your vegetables, such as dice them evenly for a tartare, slice them thinly enough for a carpaccio or make batons or spaghetti strings for a salad.

For a tartare, I recommend that you cut your vegetables into ½ cm (¼ inch) dice. Multi-functional choppers are very practical tools which make light work of this task.

Graters, as well as certain types of peelers, are also very practical for obtaining slices of vegetables thin enough to warrant being called carpaccios.

And no matter what, remember that the denser the texture of the vegetable, the better it will taste when cut thinly; so don't think twice to slice! But watch out for your fingers…

— —

MY LITTLE TIPS

When I put together my salads, I like to mix shapes, colours and textures depending on the inspiration of the moment. For example, to give an otherwise soft salad a little bit of 'bite', I might grate some semolina-like crumbs from the head of a raw cauliflower.

— —

RAW FISH: TIPS AND TECHNIQUES FROM A PRO

If I could only give one piece of advice, it would be this: use only the freshest possible fish! And just to remind you, fresh fish does not smell bad nor does it give off any odour of ammonia. It might carry the faintest scent of the sea – but nothing stronger than that.

MY LITTLE TIPS

Before buying your fish, you need to find a regular, trusty fishmonger. I know that mine would only offer me the best and I trust him completely. Don't think twice about asking your fishmonger to gut, skin and fillet the fish for you. He knows how to do this and will invariably have better tools than you for the job.

Usually, my fishmonger helps me select the best seasonal fish of the day and only then do I decide on a recipe. If I start with a fixed idea about a certain recipe and I'm intent on finding the right fish for it, I often settle for a mediocre specimen just because it fits the bill and not because I'm convinced of its beauty. Then I'm disappointed with the result!

There is a basic guideline when eating fresh fish: transfer it directly from the fishmonger's stall to your refrigerator and then to your plate on the same day. Whatever you do, don't wait a few days before eating it! And before you store it in the upper part of your refrigerator, rinse it and wrap it in greaseproof or parchment paper.

Beware of bacteria! We find it more and more in raw fish. If you are concerned about bacteria, here's a good tip: put your bought fish in the freezer for 48 hours, then let it thaw gradually in the lower part of your refrigerator, allowing a thawing period of 6-8 hours for typical fillets.

– –

TECHNIQUES

SASHIMI

Wash and dry the fish, then use tweezers to remove all the bones. With a very sharp knife, cut the fish fillets or steaks from top to bottom in sections about the width of four fingers. Cutting against the grain of the fish, divide the sections into even strips, of a width that suits your personal taste.

– –

CARPACCIO

Because the flesh of fish is so soft, it is almost impossible to cut it into very thin slices, even with a super sharp knife. The trick is to wrap the piece of fish in cling film (plastic wrap) or aluminium foil and freeze it for about one hour, so as to firm up the texture of the flesh. For slicing, use a very sharp knife with a sufficiently long blade for the task in hand. Slice the fish into very thin slices or strips and transfer them directly to individual plates or a serving platter. Cover the carpaccio with cling film until you are ready to serve it. I usually season my carpaccios at the last moment, especially if the sauce contains lemon juice. If there is no accompanying sauce, I just add lemon juice.

– –

TARTARE

Whatever you do, don't use an electric blender or chopper, unless you want to risk making baby food. For hand-ground fish, all you need are two good, well-sharpened knives. First cut the fish into large cubes, then slice through each cube with two knives held criss-cross fashion. If you cannot do this – and, yes, it takes a bit of practice – cut each cube into 1 cm (³/₈ inch) thick slices and then cut each slice into tiny dice. As with carpaccios, you can season tartares and keep them refrigerated, but when it comes to the addition of lemon juice, you can only add this at the last moment.

––

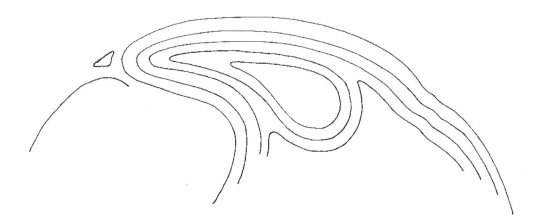

RAW MEAT

As with fishmongers and fish, I choose my butcher before choosing my meat. When I go to Mr. Louis, I know I will be getting quality meat and choice cuts from animals raised by small farmers who respect both animals and the environment.

MY LITTLE TIPS

For raw food recipes, you will not find as broad a range of options at the butcher's shop as you will at the fishmonger's. You'll have to choose between beef and veal, or duck for the more daring! Forget pork, which should not be eaten raw under any circumstance. And, personally, I'm not very partial to rabbit or lamb. Even when my Lebanese friends serve me a delicious lamb tartare, I have trouble eating more than a few bites. As far as poultry and horsemeat are concerned, I'm not a fan either, so you won't find them in this book.

A little tip for beginners: don't be fooled by the nice red colour of a steak in the meat aisle of the first supermarket you walk into. I feel I should remind you that food colouring is often used to give tired meat a fresher appearance.

It is absolutely necessary to know which products you're buying and to let the butcher know that you'll be eating them raw. Freshness is essential in order to avoid any health and safety problems because potential bacteria will not be destroyed if you do not cook the meat.

As often as possible, eat your meat the day you buy it. If it is ground beef for a tartare, it is essential that you eat it the same day or you may as well put it in the rubbish bin! To store meat properly before preparing it keep it in its original packaging of the butcher's own paper and put it in the coldest part of your fridge, which is usually the top shelf.

——

TECHNIQUES
CARPACCIO

Unless you have a professional meat slicer, it is difficult to cut fresh meat into carpaccio. I recommend that you wrap up your cut of meat and place it in the freezer for one hour before slicing it. This will firm up the texture of the flesh. For slicing, use a very sharp knife with a sufficiently long blade for the task in hand. Slice the meat into very thin slices or strips and transfer them directly to individual plates or a serving platter. Cover the carpaccio with cling film or plastic wrap and refrigerate it until you are ready to serve. I usually season my carpaccios at the last moment, especially if the sauce contains lemon juice. As an alternative, I sometimes drizzle a sauce over my carpaccio, cover it and refrigerate it. I then add the lemon juice, if it is called for, at the last moment.

Cut the meat into thin slices and arrange each slice onto a plate or serving platter as soon as it is cut. Cover the plates with cling film or plastic wrap, and refrigerate until ready to serve. Usually I only season my carpaccios at the last minute, especially if the sauce has lemon in it.

Alternative: I drizzle a sauce over my carpaccio, cover it and refrigerate it. I then add the lemon juice (if necessary) at the last minute, just before serving.

——

TARTARE

You have two choices: ground tartare, or knife-cut tartare, which refers to meat that is hand-cut into small dice. Usually people ask their butcher to grind the meat for them. But if you have a meat grinder, you can make your own 'minute tartare'! To make a knife-cut tartare, I usually prefer the most tender cut, notably the fillet or tenderloin. First remove all the nervous tissue from the meat then cut it into 1 cm (³/₈ inch) thick slices. Next, cut the slices into strips 1 cm (³/₈ inch) wide and then, finally, cut the strips into 1 cm (³/₈ inch) dice. If the meat you are cutting is beef or veal and it is very tender, you do not have to dice it into quite such small pieces. For duck, on the other hand, tiny dice are ideal. A good, well-sharpened knife is all that you'll need! As with carpaccios, you can usually season tartares, unless the seasoning contains lemon juice, as soon as they are made. You can then cover them and keep them refrigerated until needed. If lemon juice is a seasoning ingredient, you can only add this at the last moment. When making a classic steak tartare with egg yolk, you should prepare it immediately before serving.

--

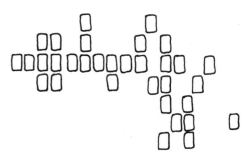

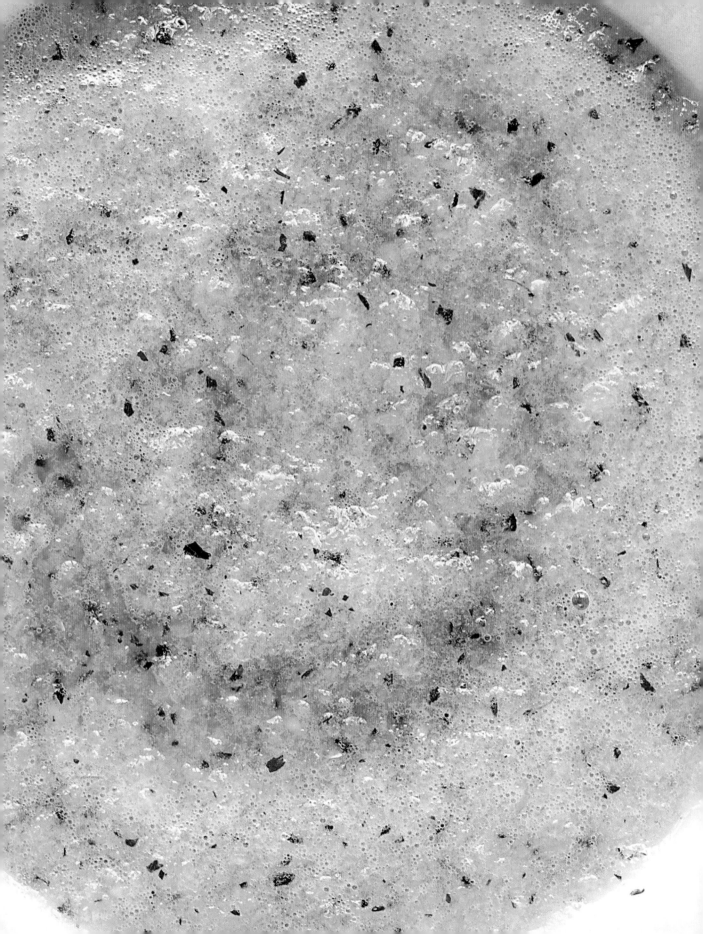

SOUPS

GREEN SOUP WITH SEEDS (100% RAW)

SERVES 4 – PREPARATION 10 MINUTES

– 2 cucumbers
– 2 courgettes/zucchini
– flesh of 2 avocados
– 300 ml (1 ¼ US / 1 AU cups) water
– juice of 2 limes
– about 5 cm (2 inches) grated fresh ginger root

TO SERVE
– 2 tsp pumpkin seeds
– 2 tsp brown linseeds
– 2 tsp brown mustard seeds
– olive oil
– fleur de sel and freshly ground pepper

Peel the cucumbers, wash the courgettes, then chop these vegetables coarsely. Using a high-performance blender or food processor, blend the chopped vegetables, avocado flesh, water, lime juice and ginger, to obtain a smooth purée. If the purée is slightly too thick for your liking, add a little more water. Cover and chill the soup in the refrigerator.

Serve in soup bowls. At the last moment, add a drizzle of olive oil, fleur de sel and pepper, then sprinkle with the 3 types of seeds, all lightly crushed with a pestle.

NOTE
The pumpkin seeds, brown linseeds and brown mustard seeds can be found in health-food stores.

SPINACH, AVOCADO AND GINGER SOUP (100% RAW)

SERVES 4-6 – PREPARATION 15 MINUTES

– 1 small or ½ large cucumber, weighing about 300 g (11 oz)
– 125 g (4 ½ oz) spinach
– flesh of 1 avocado
– 4 cm (2 inches) grated fresh ginger root
– 300 ml (1 ¼ US / 1 ¼ AU cups) water
– juice of 1 lime

TO SERVE
– 1 tsp nigella seeds (optional)
– olive oil
– sea salt and freshly ground pepper

Peel the cucumber and chop it finely. Wash the spinach and chop it roughly. Blend all of the main ingredients together to obtain a smooth purée.

Serve in soup bowls. At the last moment, add a drizzle of olive oil, sprinkle with the nigella seeds, and season with a little sea salt and a good turn of the pepper mill. You can also garnish the soup with a few small spinach leaves.

"NON RAW" VARIATION
For a more luxurious version, garnish each bowl of soup with a generous spoonful of lightly salted whipped cream; to make this, beat 100 ml (³/₈ US / ²/₅ AU cup) of cold whipping cream with a pinch of salt until you have soft peaks.

I love to sprinkle the soup with crushed hazelnuts at the last moment before serving.

SOUP OF INDIA (100% RAW)

SERVES 4 – PREPARATION 15 MINUTES

– 1 small or ¹/₂ large cucumber, weighing about 300 g (11 oz)
– 2 courgettes/zucchini
– 2 ripe tomatoes
– 6 sprigs of coriander/cilantro
– 1 tsp ground cumin
– 1 tsp ground ginger
– juice of 1 lime
– 2 tsp sesame oil
– ¹/₂ tsp fine salt

TO SERVE
– 1 tsp caraway seeds
– ¹/₂ tsp turmeric

Peel the cucumber. Slice about 50 g (2 oz) finely, and set these cucumber slices aside for the garnish. Chop the remainder of the cucumber finely. Wash the courgettes and the tomatoes and chop finely. Blend all of the main ingredients together to obtain a smooth purée. Taste and adjust seasoning if necessary.

Serve the soup in shallow bowls and garnish with the reserved cucumber slices, the caraway seeds and a sprinkling of turmeric.

SPICY SOUP (100% RAW)

SERVES 2-4 – PREPARATION 10 MINUTES

– 1 small red chilli pepper
– 400 g (14 oz) tomatoes
– 200 ml (³/₄ US / ⁴/₅ AU cups) coconut water
– flesh of ¹/₂ avocado
– 1 clove of garlic
– 4 cm (2 inches) grated fresh ginger root
– juice of 1 lime
– ¹/₂ bunch of coriander/cilantro
– 2 slices of crystalized ginger
– olive oil
– sea salt

Cut the chilli pepper in half, remove the seeds and reserve the other half for adding later if necessary. Chop the tomatoes coarsely then blend all of the ingredients together, except the crystalized ginger and olive oil, to obtain a smooth purée. Taste the soup and if you would like to increase the heat, add the other half of the reserved chilli pepper, and blend again. Cut the crystalized ginger into thin batons.

Serve in soup bowls. Top the soup with a few batons of the crystalized ginger, add a drizzle of olive oil, and sprinkle with a little sea salt.

This soup is very spicy so you may wish to serve it in small portions. For lovers of spicy food, you can garnish their bowls with some very finely chopped chilli pepper.

3C SOUP (100% RAW)

SERVES 6 — PREPARATION 10 MINUTES

– 1 small cucumber
– 2 courgettes/zucchini
– 370 ml (1 ½ US / 1 ½ AU cups) water
– 3 tsp organic soy sauce
– ½ tsp sesame oil
– leaves of ½ bunch of coriander/cilantro
– salt and freshly ground pepper

TO SERVE
– olive oil
– 3 tsp hemp seeds
– 3 tsp poppy seeds

Peel the cucumber, scrub the courgettes, then finely chop both vegetables and put them in the bowl of a food processor or blender. Add the water, the soy sauce, the sesame oil, the coriander and a little pepper. Blend to a smooth purée. Taste and adjust seasoning if necessary.

Serve the soup in shallow bowls, drizzle with olive oil and sprinkle with the seeds. This soup can be served at room temperature or cold with a little ice in the summer.

NOTE
Hempseed and poppy seeds can be found in health-food stores.

GREEN GAZPACHO (100% RAW)

SERVES 4 – PREPARATION 15 MINUTES

- 2 medium-sized cucumbers
- 1 granny smith apple
- about 6 spring onions/US scallions/AU shallots
- 2 sprigs of coriander/cilantro
- 1 sprig of mint
- 2 sprigs of basil
- 2 sprigs of parsley
- 2 cm (1 inch) fresh ginger root
- flesh of 1 avocado
- juice of 1 lime
- 2 UK/US tbsp (1 1/2 AU tbsp) olive oil
- salt and pepper

Wash the cucumber and the apple, paying attention to scrub their skins well if they are not organic. Wash the onions and the herbs. Pass the cucumber, apple, spring onions, herbs and ginger through a centrifugal juicer to obtain a juice. Blend the avocado, the lime juice and the olive oil with the vegetable and fruit juice until smooth. Season with salt and pepper. Chill the gazpacho in the refrigerator until ready to serve.

Serve the gazpacho in shallow bowls and garnish with some freshly ground pepper. If necessary, add some ice cubes to lower the temperature to your liking.

VARIATION

If you do not have a centrifugal juicer, use your favourite blender to blend the vegetables, apple and herbs with the lime juice and olive oil for a few minutes. Pass the juice through a fine-meshed sieve and then blend the avocado with the juice to finish the gazpacho.

CLASSIC GAZPACHO (100% RAW)

SERVES 4 – PREPARATION 20 MINUTES
CHILLING 2 HOURS

- – 4 tomatoes
- – 1 cucumber
- – ½ green pepper
- – ½ red pepper
- – 1 onion
- – 2 cloves of garlic
- – 2 UK/US tbsp (1 ½ AU tbsp) wine vinegar
- – 3 UK/US tbsp (2 AU tbsp plus 1 tsp) olive oil
- – salt and freshly ground pepper

TO SERVE
- – 2 sprigs of coriander/cilantro, with or without the flowers
- – olive oil

Wash the tomatoes, cucumber and peppers. Remove the seeds from the peppers and chop the vegetables coarsely. Peel and finely chop the onion and garlic cloves. Blend the chopped vegetables and garlic with the vinegar and the 3 tablespoons of olive oil. Season with salt and pepper. For an extra smooth gazpacho, you can pass the blended mixture through a fine sieve. Chill the gazpacho in the refrigerator for 2 hours or until cold.

Serve the chilled gazpacho in shallow bowls. Drizzle each helping with olive oil, sprinkle with some salt and freshly ground pepper, and garnish with fresh coriander before serving.

NOTE
Add a generous spoonful of guacamole to each bowl for an added garnish (see page 212).

CUCUMBER AND MINT SOUP (100% RAW)

SERVES 4 — PREPARATION 10 MINUTES

– 4 medium-sized cucumbers
– 4 sprigs of mint (leaves only)
– 4 UK/US tbsp (3 AU tbsp) white cream of balsamic vinegar
– 3 UK/US tbsp (2 AU tbsp plus 1 tsp) soft light brown sugar/raw caster
– freshly ground pepper

Peel the cucumbers and roughly chop them. Put them in the bowl of a food processor or blender with the mint leaves, vinegar, sugar and some freshly ground pepper. Blend well to obtain a smooth purée. Taste, and adjust seasoning if necessary.

VARIATION

If you find cream of white balsamic vinegar, it's even better for this recipe than the brown version! If you don't have either one, you can substitute another alcohol-based vinegar.

This soup is very refreshing on a beautiful summer's day!

ENERGIZING SOUP (100% RAW)

SERVES 4 – PREPARATION 15 MINUTES

– 100 g (4 oz) spinach leaves
– 1 courgette/zucchini
– 1/3 cucumber
– 1 tsp wakame seaweed powder
– 8 basil leaves
– 2 cm (1 inch) grated fresh ginger root
– 2 UK/US tbsp (1 1/2 AU tbsp) soy sauce
– 3 UK/US tbsp (2 AU tbsp plus 1 tsp) almond purée/butter
– 250 ml (1 US / 1 AU cup) water
– fleur de sel and freshly ground pepper

— —

Wash the spinach leaves and the courgette. Peel the cucumber. Coarsely chop the courgette and cucumber. To complete the soup, blend all the ingredients to a smooth purée. Taste, and adjust seasoning if necessary. If the soup is too thick for your liking, add a little more water.

NOTE
Powdered wakame seaweed and almond purée can be found in health-food stores.

This soup is very energizing. For cold winter nights, you can heat it gently in a bowl resting in some hot water in the sink. For the soup to remain "raw", make sure that its temperature does not exceed 42°C (108°F).

SALADS

SEAWEED SALAD WITH FRESH TUNA (100% RAW)

SERVES 4 – PREPARATION 10 MINUTES

– 100 g (4 oz) raw tuna steak
– 50 g (2 oz) daikon radish
– 60 g (2 ½ oz) fresh wakame seaweed
– 20 g (³/₄ oz) kombu seaweed

FOR THE DRESSING
– 2 tsp sesame oil
– 1 tsp caster sugar/superfine
– 3 tsp rice vinegar
– 3 tsp organic light soy sauce
– 3 tsp fish sauce/nuoc mam

TO SERVE
– 3 tsp sesame seeds
– 3 tsp uncooked, crushed thai rice

Prepare the dressing by mixing together the sesame oil, sugar, rice vinegar, soy sauce and the fish sauce.

Wash the tuna, pat it dry and cut it into small cubes; keep it chilled in the refrigerator. Peel the daikon radish and cut it into very small cubes. Finely slice the seaweed and combine it with the radish. Put these ingredients into a mixing bowl. Just before serving the salad, add the tuna and the dressing and mix gently to distribute the ingredients evenly. Taste and adjust seasoning if necessary. Sprinkle with sesame seeds and crushed rice. Serve immediately.

NOTE
If you cannot find fresh seaweed (available from Japanese grocers, health-food stores, and on the internet), use dehydrated seaweed and rehydrate it in a large bowl of lukewarm water for 20-30 minutes.

Daikon radish is a long, white, mild-flavoured radish from Asia.

SEED AND SPROUT TARTARE (100% RAW)

SERVES 6 – PREPARATION 30 MINUTES

- 4 firm tomatoes
- ½ yellow or orange pepper
- 1 firm courgette/zucchini
- 2 handfuls of soybean sprouts
- 2 spring onions/US scallions/AU shallots
- 3 tsp sunflower seeds
- 3 tsp pumpkin seeds/pepitas
- 3 tsp linseeds/flaxseeds
- 3 tsp pine nuts
- 20 g (¾ oz) red cabbage sprouts
- 2 sprigs of fresh mint, chopped

FOR THE DRESSING
- juice of ½ lemon
- 3 UK/US tbsp (2 AU tbsp plus 1 tsp) olive oil
- a few drops of Tabasco sauce
- fleur de sel and freshly ground pepper

TO SERVE
- 1 tsp gomasio

Wash the vegetables well, especially if they are not organic. Cut the tomatoes in half, remove the seeds, and cut into a small dice. Repeat with the pepper. Cut the courgette into a small dice, the soybean sprouts into small batons, and finely chop the spring onions. Lightly crush all the seeds and the pine nuts.

Prepare the dressing by mixing together the lemon juice with the olive oil, Tabasco sauce and a little salt and pepper.

When you are ready to serve the salad, toss all of the vegetables with the seeds and nuts, the red cabbage sprouts and the mint. Add the dressing and mix well. Sprinkle with the gomasio and add some freshly ground pepper. Serve immediately.

NOTE
You can find gomasio in health-food stores. You can prepare the vegetable mixture in advance and keep it fresh in an airtight container. However, it's best to chop the fresh mint and garnish the salad just before serving.

CABBAGE ROLLS WITH TWO SAUCES ⓘ(100% RAW)

FOR 10 ROLLS – PREPARATION 25 MINUTES

CHILLING 1 HOUR

– 10 small (collard greens, kale, savoy cabbage...)
– cabbage leaves
– 100 g (4 oz) daikon radish
– 1/2 carrot
– 1/4 cucumber
– 1/2 mango
– flesh of 1/2 avocado
– 20 g (3/4 oz) radish sprouts (optional)
– 2 UK/US tbsp (1 1/2 AU tbsp) sesame seeds

FOR SAUCE #1
– 70 g (3 oz) crunchy peanut butter
– 1 pitted and finely chopped date
– 1/2 crushed clove of garlic
– 1 tsp soy sauce
– 1 pinch (hot variety) chili powder
– water

FOR SAUCE #2
– 4 tsp white miso
– 1 crushed clove of garlic
– about 2 cm (1 inch) grated fresh ginger root
– 4 tsp lime juice
– 2 tsp sesame purée/tahini
– 4 tsp water

—————————————————————————————————

Wash and dry the cabbage leaves. Peel and grate the daikon radish and the carrot. Wash the cucumber well and cut it into batons along with the mango and the avocado. Place some radish, carrot, mango, avocado and cucumber along the outer edge of each cabbage leaf and sprinkle with sesame seeds and radish sprouts if you are including them. Roll up the leaves, cover the rolls with cling film (plastic wrap) and chill in the refrigerator for at least 1 hour.

To prepare the sauces: mix together all of the ingredients for each sauce, adding a little water to sauce #1 if it is too thick.

Serve the cabbage rolls with the two sauces for dipping.

NOTE

White miso and tahini (sesame purée) can be found at health-food stores.

ALL GREEN SPRING SALAD (100% RAW)

SERVES 6 – PREPARATION 15 MINUTES

- 4 asparagus spears
- 3 tsp petit pois/French baby peas
- 1 small firm courgette/zucchini
- 1 handful of baby spinach
- 20 g (¾ oz) radish sprouts

FOR THE DRESSING
- 2 UK/US tbsp (1½ AU tbsp) rapeseed/canola oil
- 2 UK/US tbsp (1½ AU tbsp) olive oil
- fleur de sel and freshly ground pepper

TO SERVE
- 4 sprigs of coriander/cilantro, leaves torn

Wash the vegetables well, especially if they are not organic. Peel away any tough skin from the asparagus spears. Cut off the stalk-end if it is tough. Use a vegetable peeler to slice the spears lengthways into paper-thin ribbons working from the end to tip. Crush the peas lightly with a fork. Finely slice or peel the courgette lengthways into long strips. In a large bowl, toss all the vegetables with the sprouts.

Prepare the dressing by mixing together the two oils with a little salt and pepper. To serve, drizzle the dressing over the salad and garnish with fresh coriander.

VARIATION

For an iodine-rich version, garnish the salad with a packet of dried bonito flakes just before serving. Dried bonito flakes can be found at Japanese grocers. Radish sprouts can be found in health-food stores.

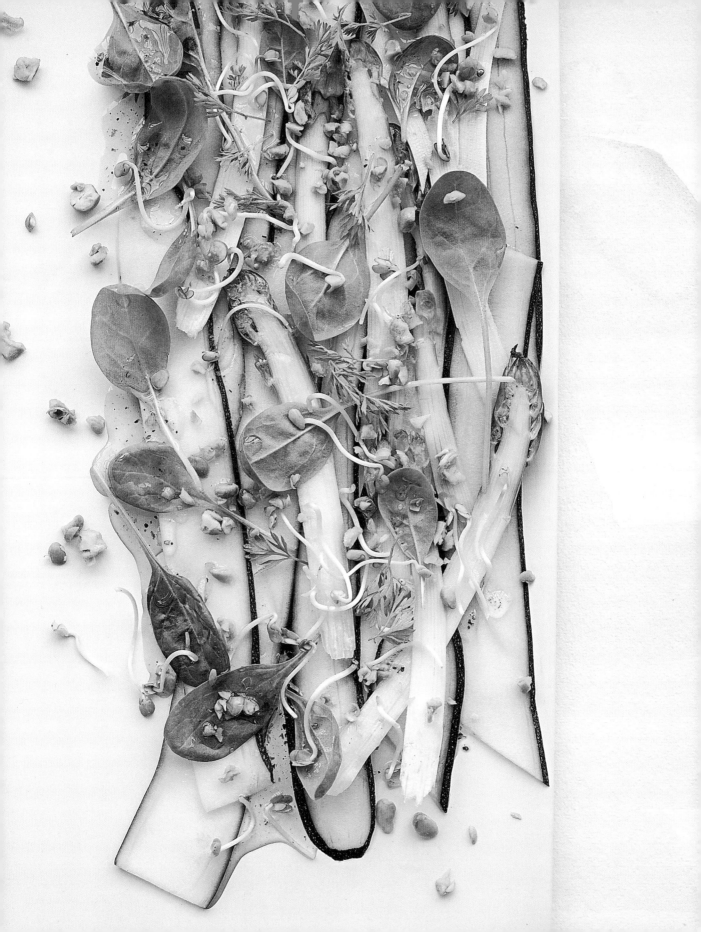

RAW TALENT ALEXANDRE DROUARD &
SAMUEL NAHON – TERROIRS D'AVENIR
It's a dazzling partnership. Both men are
innovative, driven and gifted. Thanks to them,
the local produce of France arrives directly on
our plates.

TERROIRS D'AVENIR
7 rue du Nil
75002 Paris

WILD WINTER SALAD

SERVES 4 – PREPARATION 20 MINUTES

- 1 lemon
- 50 g (2 oz) black radish (you can substitute red radish)
- 100 g (4 oz) kohlrabi
- 100 g (4 oz) uncooked beetroot/beet, the colour of your choice
- 150 g (5 oz) carrots, the colour of your choice
- 1 apple
- 100 g (4 oz) white cabbage
- 50 g (2 oz) fennel
- 100 g (4 oz) chicory/Belgian endive/witlof
- 1 celery stick/stalk

- 50 g (2 oz) white button mushrooms
- 2 spring onions/US scallions/AU shallots
- 2 UK/US tbsp (1 ½ AU tbsp) garlic vinegar, preferably made from wild, or bear, garlic
- 5 UK/US tbsp (4 AU tbsp plus 1 tsp) olive oil, preferably the Kalamata variety from Greece
- Espelette pepper or other mild chilli pepper
- fleur de sel and freshly ground pepper

Squeeze the juice from the lemon and put it in a small bowl or jug. Wash and peel the radish, kohlrabi, beetroot, carrots and the apple. Grate these items coarsely into strips. Sprinkle the grated kohlrabi and apple with about half of the lemon juice to prevent discoloration. Put all the grated vegetables in a large salad bowl.

Wash the white cabbage, fennel, chicory and celery. Remove any earth from the stems of the mushrooms, then rinse them rapidly and wipe them dry. Use a mandoline or very sharp knife to cut these vegetables into fine slices. Sprinkle the sliced mushrooms with the remaining lemon juice. Transfer all the sliced vegetables to the salad bowl. Trim, wash and chop the spring onions finely then mix these into the assembled salad.

For the salad dressing, combine the vinegar and oil in a small bowl, stirring to blend. Drizzle the dressing over the salad. Sprinkle with fleur de sel, a little freshly ground pepper and a pinch of Espelette pepper. Toss the ingredients to distribute flavours evenly, then serve immediately.

NOTE – KOHLRABI

This green and sometimes purple vegetable lends itself beautifully to raw food dishes, adding a splendid crunch as well as a soft spicy taste. To prepare, wash the kohlrabi and set aside its lovely edible leaves. Use a very sharp knife to trim away the base and the top. Continue to use the knife to peel it, making sure to remove the fibrous layer just under the surface. The best way to enjoy raw kohlrabi is sliced as thinly as possible, carpaccio style.

TOMATOES WITH GINGER AND SOY VINAIGRETTE (100% RAW)

SERVES 4 – PREPARATION 15 MINUTES

MARINATING 1 NIGHT

CHILLING 2 HOURS

– 400 g (14 oz) tomatoes of various colours and varieties

FOR THE VINAIGRETTE DRESSING
– 4 cm (1 ¼ inches) fresh ginger root, or more if desired
– 3 tsp organic soy sauce
– 6 UK/US tbsp (4 ½ AU tbsp) olive oil
– salt and freshly ground pepper

_____

Choose the most beautiful ripe tomatoes of the season, preferably grown organically. Make the vinaigrette dressing the night before serving the salad: peel and grate the ginger and put it in a small jar along with the soy sauce and the olive oil. Tighten the lid of the jar, shake the mixture and chill it over night.

About two hours before serving the salad, wash and dry the tomatoes. Cut them into quarters or wedges, aiming to have pieces that are more or less of the same size. Transfer the tomatoes to a large bowl or serving dish. Remove the dressing from the refrigerator and pour it through a fine sieve set over a small bowl, discarding the solids of ginger. Drizzle the strained dressing over the tomatoes, cover, and transfer to the refrigerator.

Just before serving, season the tomatoes with salt and a few turns of the pepper mill.

VARIATION
You can also slice the tomatoes if you don't want to cut wedge shapes. For a more gingery taste, add a few little matchsticks of fresh ginger – and add them again and again as you wish!

ASPARAGUS WITH CURED HAM AND CHEESE

SERVES 4 – PREPARATION 15 MINUTES

– 1 bunch of young asparagus spears
– 20 g (³/₄ oz) red cheese such as Mimolette, Red Leicester, or other
  hard cheese such as Gruyere
– 4 slices of Italian dry-cured ham such as speck or prosciutto
– 4-5 chives
– 1-2 tbsp maple syrup
– 4 UK/US tbsp (3 AU tbsp) olive oil
– salt and freshly ground pepper

Wash the asparagus spears, cut off any woody ends and peel away any tough fibres from the stalks. Arrange the spears on a large serving dish and set aside briefly. Wash and dry the chives and set aside.

Use a vegetable peeler or a small sharp knife to take long shavings from the cheese and lay these over the spears. Cut the ham into pieces of a similar size to the cheese and distribute them on top. Snip the chives and scatter the pieces over the assembly.

In a small bowl, make a simple dressing by stirring together the olive oil and maple syrup. Season the dressing with salt and pepper to taste, then drizzle it over the salad. Serve immediately.

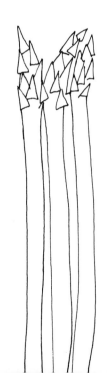

GRATED WHITE RADISH WITH THAI SAUCE (100% RAW)

SERVES 4 — PREPARATION 15 MINUTES

– 350 g (12 ½ oz) white Daikon radish
– ⅓ bunch of coriander/cilantro

FOR THE DRESSING
– ½ small red chilli pepper
– juice and zest of 1 organic lime
– 1 tsp maple syrup
– 3 tsp nuoc mam sauce
– 1 tsp soy sauce
– 3 tsp sunflower oil
– 1 tsp sesame oil

TO SERVE
– lime zest taken from the lime for the sauce
– 3 tsp chopped peanuts

Peel the radish, grate it finely and put it in a bowl. Wash and dry the coriander, then snip or coarsely chop the leaves and add them to the bowl; set aside briefly.

To make the dressing, start by slicing the chilli pepper in half, rinsing away the seeds, then chopping the chilli very finely. If you like, you can protect your hands while you do this, preferably wearing gloves; alternatively wash your hands well after handling the chilli. Zest the lime and set the zest aside for the garnish. Squeeze the lime for its juice. Mix together in a small bowl the lime juice, maple syrup, nuoc mam sauce, soy sauce, sunflower oil and sesame oil. Stir in the chopped chilli pepper.

Just before serving, toss the salad in the sauce, turning the ingredients to coat them evenly. Serve the salad from a bowl or from individual serving plates. Scatter over the chopped peanuts and the reserved lime zest, and serve straight away.

TABOULEH SALAD WITH SPROUTS (100% RAW)

SERVES 6 – PREPARATION 25 MINUTES

CHILLING 3 HOURS

– 40 g (1 1/2 oz) bulgur or couscous,
  preferably wholemeal
– 1 cauliflower
– 1 small cucumber
– 2 small mild-tasting onions
– 20 g (3/4 oz) red cabbage sprouts
– 4 sprigs of mint
– 4 sprigs of flat leaf parsley
– freshly ground pepper

FOR THE DRESSING
– juice of 1 lemon
– 3 UK/US tbsp (2 AU tbsp plus 1 tsp) rapeseed oil
– 2 UK/US tbsp (1 1/2 AU tbsp) hazelnut oil

Prepare the bulgur or couscous according to the directions on the packet; set aside.

To assemble the salad, wash the cauliflower and separate it into small florets, discarding the core. Using a grater or a mandoline, grate the florets into semolina-like crumbs and drop these into a large mixing bowl. Wash the cucumber, keeping its skin if it is organic but peeling it if not. Slice it in half lengthways and scoop out the seeds. Cut the flesh into small cubes; add these to the bowl. Peel and finely chop the onions. Wash and thoroughly dry the sprouts. Add the onions and sprouts to the bowl along with the bulgur. Toss these ingredients to distribute them evenly.

To prepare the dressing, mix together the lemon juice with the two oils in a small bowl. Drizzle the dressing over the salad and toss the ingredients again to coat them evenly. Cover and chill in the refrigerator for 3 hours, turning the ingredients from time to time.

Just before serving, wash and dry the herbs then chop or snip them and add them to the salad. Season to taste with freshly ground pepper.

My friend Annie replaces the grain used here with couscous maize rice. It can usually be found in health-food stores but, failing that, is available online.

RAW BEETROOT, NUT AND GRAPEFRUIT SALAD (100% RAW)

SERVES 4 – PREPARATION 15 MINUTES

MARINATING 2 HOURS

- 4 uncooked small beetroots/beets
- 1 organic grapefruit
- 1 shallot
- 4 sprigs of flat leaf parsley
- 3 tsp chopped walnuts

- 3 tsp chopped pecans
- 4 UK/US tbsp (3 AU tbsp) olive oil
- 1 tsp cream of balsamic vinegar
- salt and freshly ground pepper

Peel the beetroots – wearing gloves if you like to prevent your hands from becoming pink. Cut the beetroots into fine cubes; set aside in a bowl. Cut the grapefruit in half. Squeeze one half for its juice and save the other for zest to garnish. Pour the juice over the cubes of beetroot, cover and chill for 2 hours in the refrigerator.

Peel and finely chop the shallot. Wash, dry and coarsely chop the parsley. Strain off excess beetroot juice, but leave enough juice to keep the beetroot wet; return it to its original bowl. Add the shallot, parsley, the chopped nuts, the olive oil, the cream of balsamic vinegar, and salt and freshly ground pepper. Mix thoroughly.

To serve, distribute the beetroot tartare salad to individual serving plates. Use a fine zesting tool to scrape pith-free zest from the reserved half of grapefruit over each helping. Serve straight away.

NOTE

It is important to scrape away the zest from the grapefruit using a very fine grater, otherwise the zest may carry some inner white pith, which has a bitter taste. I use a brand called Microplane which is really great for all sorts of grating tasks, no matter what.

You can make your own cream of balsamic vinegar: put two cups of balsamic vinegar into a medium to large saucepan. Note the quantity and the level of vinegar in the pan using a toothpick or the handle of a wooden spoon. Aim to reduce the quantity to between one-third and one-half of the original amount. If the reduction concentrates to less than one-third, it can easily turn to caramel. Set the pan, uncovered, over medium heat and let the vinegar boil lightly until it has reduced to the desired level, checking progress after 15 minutes. Once you have the correct level, stand the base of the pan in iced water to arrest the cooking. Transfer the cooled reduction to an airtight container, preferably a squeezy plastic bottle.

A passionate, cutting-edge chef with a great
gift for raw food of effortless simplicity.

BONES
43 rue Godefroy Cavaignac
75011 Paris

SPICY SCALLOPS
WITH SORREL JUICE

SERVES 6 – PREPARATION 20 MINUTES
MARINATING 1¹/₂ HOURS

– 9 very fresh scallops
– 1 small kohlrabi, washed and with its
  surrounding leaves in place (see note on
  page 49)
– a few washed sorrel leaves
– a few washed dandelion leaves
– 3 tsp poppyseeds
– juice of ¹/₂ lemon
– olive oil
– a few pinches of caster sugar/superfine
– salt

FOR THE SORREL JUICE
– 2 bunches of washed and torn sorrel leaves
– ¹/₂ bunch of washed coriander/cilantro

– 30 g (1 oz) peeled and coarsely chopped
  fresh ginger
– 30 g (1 oz) coarsely chopped shallot
– 1 peeled and coarsely chopped garlic clove
– 200 ml (⁷/₈ US cup / ⁴/₅ AU cup) mineral water

FOR THE MARINATED SHALLOT
– 1 peeled and finely sliced shallot
– 1 tsp white Banyuls vinegar (you can substitute
  sherry vinegar)
– 1 tsp sparkling mineral water
– ¹/₂ tsp caster sugar/superfine
– ¹/₂ tsp of fleur de sel or salt of your choice

To prepare the marinated shallot, put the shallot in a small dish then add the vinegar, sparkling mineral water, sugar and salt. Cover the dish and leave the shallot to marinate in a cool place or the refrigerator for 1 hour.

Meanwhile, rinse the scallops and pat them dry. Put them in a dish and sprinkle with a few pinches of sugar and salt. Cover and marinate in the refrigerator for 30 minutes.

To make the sorrel juice, put the sorrel leaves, coriander, ginger, shallot, garlic, mineral water and a pinch of salt in the bowl of a blender or food processor. Pulse the ingredients just long enough to obtain a homogenous purée – no more than one minute, otherwise the juice will turn brown. Strain the juice through a fine sieve and set aside in a cool place.

When you are almost ready to serve the dish, pick off the leaves from the kohlrabi and reserve them. Peel the kohlrabi, then use a mandoline or a sharp knife to cut it into paper-thin slices. Wipe the scallops and cut them into the thinnest possible slices. Arrange the scallops on 4 serving plates with shallow bowls. Garnish each plate with 3 slices of the kohlrabi and a couple of its leaves. Add to each a few sorrel and dandelion leaves, and about 3 slices of the marinated shallot. Sprinkle with poppy seeds. Immediately before serving, add to each helping about 2 ¹/₂ – 3 tablespoons of the sorrel juice, a drizzle of olive oil and a few drops of lemon juice.

LIVELY TOMATOES WITH PARMESAN

SERVES 4 – PREPARATION 15 MINUTES

– 400 g (14 oz) tomatoes of various colours
– 25 g (1 oz) Parmesan

FOR THE VINAIGRETTE DRESSING
– 4 UK/US tbsp (3 AU tbsp) olive oil
– 3 tsp maple syrup
– salt and freshly ground pepper

Choose the most beautiful, ripe tomatoes of the season. Wash them well and dry them. Cut them into halves or wedges, aiming to have pieces that are more or less the same size. Transfer the tomatoes to a large bowl.

To make the vinaigrette dressing, mix together the olive oil and maple syrup in a small bowl. Toss the tomatoes gently in the dressing. Season to taste with salt and pepper. Serve the tomato salad from a bowl or from individual serving plates. Just before serving, use a vegetable peeler or a small sharp knife to take shavings from the Parmesan, and scatter these on top.

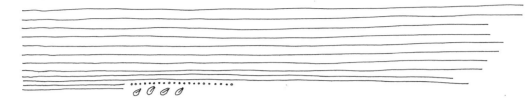

YELLOW COURGETTE SALAD WITH CRUNCH

SERVES 4 – PREPARATION 15 MINUTES

– 2 yellow courgettes/zucchini, or 4 if they are small
– 2 sprigs of mint, leaves removed
– 2 UK/US tbsp (1 1/2 AU tbsp) crushed hazelnuts
– 50 g (2 oz) pecorino

FOR THE DRESSING
– 2 UK/US tbsp (1 1/2 AU tbsp) olive oil
– 3 tsp pumpkinseed oil
– 3 tsp hazelnut oil
– salt and freshly ground pepper

Prepare the dressing by mixing together the oils with a little salt and pepper. Pour half of the dressing onto a large serving platter that can accommodate all of the courgettes once they are sliced into rounds and spread out. Reserve the remaining dressing for drizzling on top of the salad.

Wash the courgettes, scrubbing their skins well. Slice the courgettes into very thin rounds using a mandoline or a well-sharpened knife. Spread the courgette slices onto the serving platter and sprinkle with mint leaves and the crushed hazelnuts. Drizzle with the remaining dressing. Grate some large shavings of pecorino cheese on top and serve immediately.

VARIATION
You can replace the pecorino with Parmesan cheese or, alternatively, the salad is also very good without cheese. For a version less "raw", you can toast the hazelnuts for a few seconds in a skillet. You can also add some pine nuts… wonderful!

NOTE
Pumpkinseed oil can be found in health-food stores.

I plant courgettes in my garden… Yum! I harvest them while they are still small… Just so delicious!

VEGETABLE CARPACCIO (100% RAW)

SERVES 4-6 – PREPARATION 30 MINUTES

MARINATING 2 HOURS

- 16 slices of black radish
- 1 turnip
- 1 purple carrot
- 1 orange carrot
- 2 jerusalem artichokes
- 4 florets of cauliflower
- 2 florets of broccoli
- 1 small yellow courgette/zucchini
- 1 small uncooked yellow beetroot

FOR THE MARINADE
- juice of 1 lemon
- 2 UK/US tbsp (1 1/2 AU tbsp) soft light brown sugar/raw caster

- 3 UK/US tbsp (2 AU tbsp plus 1 tsp) rapeseed canola oil
- 4 1/2 tsp hazelnut oil
- 4 1/2 tsp olive oil

TO SERVE
- sea salt and freshly ground pepper
- 2 UK/US tbsp (1 1/2 AU tbsp) chopped hazelnuts
- 2 sprigs of basil

- -

Wash all of the vegetables well, especially if they are not organic. Peel the black radish, turnip, carrots and the Jerusalem artichokes. With a mandoline, or very sharp knife, finely slice all of the vegetables for the carpaccio and place them on a large plate, in one layer if possible.

In a small bowl, mix the lemon juice with the sugar and the oils. Pour the marinade onto the sliced vegetables. Cover with cling film (plastic wrap) and transfer to the refrigerator for at least 2 hours. Turn the vegetables once or twice while they are marinating.

Just before serving, sprinkle the vegetable carpaccio lightly with sea salt, pepper, and the chopped hazelnuts. Garnish with fresh basil leaves.

VARIATION
If you have the time, let the vegetables marinate in the refrigerator overnight.

If you can't find a yellow beetroot, you can substitute a red one.

FENNEL AND PECORINO
SERVES 6 – PREPARATION 20 MINUTES

- 2-3 bulbs of fennel, depending on the size
- ¹/₂ lemon confit
- 4 small gherkins/dill pickles
- 20 caperberries or capers
- 6 sprigs of flat-leafed parsley
- 25 g (1 oz) peppered pecorino

FOR THE DRESSING
- juice of 1 lemon
- 1 ¹/₂ tsp mustard
- 1 ¹/₂ tsp crème fraîche/sour cream
- 4 ¹/₂ tbsp wine vinegar
- 4 UK/US tbsp (3 AU tbsp) olive oil
- freshly ground pepper

Cut the fennel bulbs into thin batons with a sharp knife or a mandoline. Wash the batons and drain them. Rinse the lemon confit with water and finely chop; discard any seeds. Thinly slice the gherkins into rounds. In a large bowl, combine the fennel, lemon confit, gherkins, caperberries and the parsley.

In a small bowl, mix the lemon juice with the mustard, crème fraîche, vinegar, olive oil and a little pepper. Drizzle this dressing over the salad and toss to coat ingredients evenly. Keep the salad chilled in the refrigerator until ready to serve.

Just before serving, garnish each salad with shavings of peppered pecorino cheese.

FENNEL, OLIVES AND CHILLI PEPPER (100% RAW)

SERVES 6 – PREPARATION 25 MINUTES

- 2-3 bulbs of fennel, depending on the size
- 2 UK/US tbsp (1 ½ AU tbsp) pitted black olives
- 1 chilli pepper
- 2 cloves of garlic

FOR THE DRESSING
- 6 cherry tomatoes
- juice of ½ lime
- 4 UK/US tbsp (3 AU tbsp) olive oil
- fleur de sel and freshly ground pepper

Cut the fennel bulbs into thin batons with a sharp knife or a mandoline. Wash the batons and drain them. Thinly slice the olives into rounds. Cut the chilli pepper in half, discard the seeds, and finely chop it. Very finely chop the garlic cloves. In a large bowl, mix the fennel with the olives, chilli pepper and garlic.

Make a dressing by blending together the tomatoes, the lime juice, the olive oil and a little salt and pepper. Drizzle the dressing over the salad and toss to combine. Keep the salad chilled in the refrigerator until you are ready to serve it.

RAINBOW BEETROOT CARPACCIO (100% RAW)

SERVES 4 – PREPARATION 15 MINUTES

– 300 g (11 oz) uncooked beetroots of various colours
　 (yellow or golden, rainbow, white, or red)
– fennel flowers (optional)

FOR THE DRESSING
– 3 tsp hazelnut oil
– 3 tsp pumpkinseed oil
– 3 tsp olive oil
– 3 tsp cream of white balsamic vinegar
– fleur de sel and freshly ground pepper

– –

As raw beetroot might stain your hands, you may choose to put on some rubber gloves. Wash the beetroots and peel them. With a sharp knife, or better still, a mandoline – slice them as thinly as possible. Transfer the slices to a large bowl.

Prepare a dressing by combining the oils and the balsamic cream with a little salt and pepper. Drizzle the dressing over the salad and toss to combine. Garnish with the fennel flowers (optional).

NOTE
If you can't find beetroots of unusual colours, you can use classic red ones.

CHINESE CABBAGE WITH DRIED BONITO (100% RAW)

SERVES 4 — PREPARATION 15 MINUTES

– 2 small heads of pak choi/bok choy
– 4 UK/US tbsp (3 AU tbsp) chopped cashew nuts
– 2 UK/US tbsp (1 ½ AU tbsp) dried bonito flakes

FOR THE VINAIGRETTE DRESSING
– 3 tsp tahini
– 2 UK/US tbsp (1 ½ AU tbsp) umeboshi
  (Japanese plum) vinegar
– 2 UK/US tbsp (1 ½ AU tbsp) hazelnut oil

To prepare the dressing, mix the tahini, the umeboshi vinegar and the hazelnut oil in a small bowl; set aside briefly.

Cut a thick slice from the root of each head of pak choi, so as to separate their stalks complete with their leaves. Wash and dry the stalks and leaves. Cut them into strips about 1 cm (3/8 inch) wide, then transfer them to a large salad bowl. Mix the coarsely chopped cashew nuts into the strips of pak choi, then toss the mixture in the dressing. At the very last moment, incorporate the bonito flakes and serve immediately.

NOTE

The type of Chinese cabbage used here assumes various names: pak choi in the UK and Australia, for example, and bok choy in the US. It appears in most countries in large supermarkets, as well as in Asian grocers. The dried bonito flakes can also usually be found in Asian grocers but if you draw a blank, then you can certainly source them from internet sites.

An Asian grocer is also a likely place to find the deliciously sweet umeboshi Japanese plum vinegar. True, you can replace it for the recipe here with 3 teaspoons of raspberry vinegar, but the result will have a sharper edge. If you are unable to access either of these vinegars, then try adding a little white balsamic vinegar instead.

GRATED CELERIAC AND APPLE SALAD

SERVES 6 – PREPARATION 20 MINUTES

– I small celeriac
– 2 very ripe apples
– I large or 2 smaller limes

FOR THE DRESSING
– 2 UK/US tbsp (I ½ AU tbsp) tahini
– 2 UK/US tbsp (I ½ AU tbsp) organic soy sauce
– 4 UK/US tbsp (3 AU tbsp) walnut oil

– 2 UK/US tbsp (I ½ AU tbsp) olive oil
– salt and freshly ground pepper

TO SERVE
– 3 tsp shelled and chopped pistachios
– I ½ - 2 tbsp chopped raisins
– 40 g (I ½ oz) sheep's milk cheese, preferably tomme de brebis

---

Have ready a bowl large enough to contain the celeriac and apple. Squeeze the juice from the lime(s) and put it in the bowl – this will prevent the celeriac and apple from turning brown as you work. Peel and grate the celeriac, then peel, core, and grate the apples, dropping the grated pieces into the juice and immersing them.

In a separate bowl, mix together the tahini, the soy sauce and the oils. Taste, and adjust seasoning with pepper and salt to taste, bearing in mind the soy is already salty. Pour the sauce over the celeriac and apple mixture and toss to distribute the ingredients evenly. Cover the salad and transfer it to the refrigerator until you are almost ready to serve it.

Serve the salad from a bowl or from individual serving plates. To complete the salad, scatter it with the chopped pistachios and raisins. Use a peeler to scrape shavings from the cheese and distribute these on top. Serve without delay.

NOTE
Tahini is a purée, or paste, made from ground sesame seeds. Nowadays, it is widely available in supermarkets. If the sheep's milk cheese tomme de brebis proves difficult to find, you can substitute a firm, fruity, nutty cow's milk cheese, such as Gruyere, Emmental or Appenzeller.

VEGETABLE SALAD
WITH BOTTARGA (100% RAW)

SERVES 4 – PREPARATION 20 MINUTES

– 1 courgette/zucchini
– 4 asparagus spears
– 1 purple carrot
– 1 yellow turnip
– 1 small beetroot
– 40 g (1 1/2 oz) peeled bottarga/dried cured fish roe (optional)

FOR THE DRESSING
– 2 UK/US tbsp (1 1/2 AU tbsp) canola oil
– 2 UK/US tbsp (1 1/2 AU tbsp) olive oil
– sea salt and freshly ground pepper

––

Wash all the vegetables, scrubbing them especially well if they are not organic. Peel all of the vegetables except for the courgette. With a sharp knife or a mandoline, slice all of the vegetables lengthways as thinly as possible. For the asparagus, cut off the ends if they are woody and peel away any tough skin. Use a vegetable peeler to peel the spears end to tip into long ribbons. Arrange the vegetables on a large plate.

Combine the oils and drizzle them over the salad. Sprinkle the salad with a little sea salt and freshly ground pepper. If you are including the bottarga, use a very sharp knife or vegetable peeler to make shavings and sprinkle on top of the vegetables. Serve immediately.

NOTE
Bottarga is cured roe of grey mullet, tuna or swordfish and many regions around the Mediterranean make different variations of this.

You can prepare the seasoned vegetables in advance and keep in the refrigerator for a few hours. Garnish with the bottarga just before serving.

PAD THAI SALAD ALL RAW (100% RAW)

SERVES 4 – PREPARATION 25 MINUTES

– 100 g (4 oz) young spinach leaves
– 1 small daikon radish
– 300 g (11 oz) asparagus
– ½ red or green pepper
– 2 spring onions/US scallions/AU shallots
– 100 g (4 oz) spinach
– ⅓ bunch chopped coriander/cilantro

FOR THE DRESSING
– 2 UK/US tbsp (1 ½ AU tbsp) olive oil
– 2 UK/US tbsp (1 ½ AU tbsp) apple cider vinegar

– 1 garlic clove, crushed to a fine pulp
– juice and zest of 1 lime
– 1 tsp organic soy sauce
– 2 pinches of chilli pepper
– sea salt and freshly ground pepper

TO SERVE
– 2 UK/US tbsp (1 ½ AU tbsp) cashew nuts

_____

To prepare the salad ingredients, wash the spinach leaves and leave them to drain in a colander. Peel the daikon radish. Using a mandoline fitted with a spiral disk, cut the radish into spaghetti strings. Alternatively, you can use a sharp knife to cut the radish into very thin long strips. Wash the asparagus, trim it free of tough skin then either cut it into small pieces or slice the spears it into long thin ribbons using a vegetable peeler. Put the radish and asparagus in a large bowl. Wash the pepper, remove its seeds and finely chop it. Trim the spring onions and chop them finely from bulb to tail. Add the chopped pepper and onions to the bowl. Pat the spinach leaves dry and add them to the salad ingredients along with the coriander. Toss all the ingredients to combine them.

For the dressing, mix together in a small bowl the olive oil and the vinegar. Add the garlic stirring or whisking to blend smoothly. Stir in the lime juice and zest, soy sauce and chilli pepper. Add a little salt and pepper to taste. Pour the dressing over the salad ingredients and toss well to coat the ingredients evenly. Chop the cashew nuts coarsely and either scatter them on top of the salad or offer them separately.

NOTE
Traditionally, Pad Thai calls to mind the fried rice noodle dishes commonly served as street food in Thailand. A typical Pad Thai also includes some simple raw ingredients – such as radish, herbs and bean sprouts, which are available on the day. This flexibility extends to the Pad Thai here. Depending on season and taste, you can vary the vegetables at will. Raw grated or thinly sliced courgettes/zucchini are good for this Pad Thai, as are sweet potato spaghetti strings, bean sprouts and slices of radish of all kinds. Another useful everyday option is petits pois/French baby peas.

JUICES

CUCUMBER AND
SPINACH JUICE (100% RAW)

MAKES 2 GLASSES — PREPARATION 5 MINUTES

– 150 g (5 ½ oz) wild spinach
– 1 organic cucumber
– 100 g (4 oz) baby spinach leaves
– juice of 1 lime

Wash both types of spinach and the cucumber. Chop the wild spinach and cucumber coarsely. Pass all the ingredients through the juicer of your choice, ideally a masticating juicer (see page 10). Drink the juice straight away.

NOTE
It is best to peel the cucumber if it is not organic. It is always necessary to wash the main ingredients to be juiced, especially if they have not been grown organically. The type of edible wild spinach referred in this recipe is also known as lambsquarters, fat-hen and pigweed (Bot chenopodium album). It is exceptionally rich in oxalic acid. If you can't find any growing locally, you can either substitute wheat grass or simply add extra spinach leaves of a regular kind.

CARROT, CUCUMBER AND ALFALFA JUICE (100% RAW)

MAKES 2 GLASSES — PREPARATION 5 MINUTES

– 100 g (4 oz) carrots
– organic 150 g (5 ½ oz) cucumber
– 60 g (2 ½ oz) alfalfa spouts
– 160 g (5 ½ oz) sunflower sprouts
– 25 g (1 oz) flat leaf parsley

Wash and prepare the ingredients, scrubbing the carrots well if you are retaining their skin, and peeling the cucumber if it is not organic. Chop the carrots and cucumber coarsely. Pass all the ingredients through the juicer of your choice, ideally a masticating juicer (see page 10). Drink the juice straight away.

NOTE
More than a juice, this is an extra-strong shot of herbs and goodness!

GOOD TO KNOW
Sprouts are sprouting seeds which have been germinated under special conditions so that a shoot develops quickly. Their vitamin content is highly concentrated. You can grow your own sprouts at home and you will find information on many websites to assist you. You can now buy alfalfa sprouts in many supermarkets and most health-food stores. Sunflower sprouts may be a little more difficult to obtain locally but they are widely available online.

CABBAGE, CELERY AND HERB JUICE (100% RAW)

MAKES 2 GLASSES — PREPARATION 5 MINUTES

– 150 g (5 oz) Savoy cabbage leaves
– 120 g (4 ½ oz) celery
– 60 g (2 ½ oz) sprouts of your choice, such as alfalfa spouts
– 120 g (4 ½ oz) mixed herbs of your choice, such as flat leaf parsley, chervil, dill, tarragon

Wash the ingredients and chop the cabbage and celery coarsely. Pass all the ingredients through the juicer of your choice, ideally a masticating juicer (see page 10). Drink the juice straight away.

NOTE
Take care with the blend of herbs you choose: remember that dill, tarragon and mint are very assertive in taste and must always be used sparingly, whereas parsley and chervil are mild-natured and can be used liberally.

MAUD ZILNIK – EPICERIE GENERALE
This small organic delicatessen is very Parisian.
Everything looks beautiful and tastes good.
It's the perfect place for a spot of lunch and
for tasting and trying interesting produce of
the highest quality.

- - - - - - - - - - - - - - - -

EPICERIE GENERALE
43 rue de Verneuil
75007 Paris

MAUD'S TONIC

MAKES 4 GLASSES – PREPARATION 5 MINUTES
SOAKING 1 HOUR

– 2 good handfuls of blanched whole almonds
– 2 good handfuls of young spinach leaves
– 2 bunches of flat leaf parsley
– 2 small bunches of white seedless grapes
– 2 kiwi fruits
– 2 apples

- -

Soak the almonds in a bowl of luke-warm water for 1 hour.

Wash and drain the spinach, parsley and grapes and set them aside briefly. Peel
the kiwis and cut them into quarters. Cut the apples into quarters then peel and
core them.

Drain the almonds. Put all the ingredients, in stages, into the bowl of a high-
performance food processor or blender. Pulse the mixture briefly several times
with a pause in between to avoid over-heating the ingredients. When you have
achieved a smooth blend, drink the juice straight away.

VARIATION
You can also use a centrifugal juicer in which case you have no need to peel and
core the apples. On the other hand, you must always peel the kiwis.

A LITTLE MORE
If you do not have a powerful enough food processor or blender to break down
the firm texture of the apples and almonds to a sufficiently fine purée, you can
strain the chunkier purée that your machine produces through a fine sieve, then
blend it again to obtain a smooth juice.

AVOCADO, CUCUMBER AND COCONUT SMOOTHIE (100% RAW)

MAKES 4 GLASSES — PREPARATION 5 MINUTES

– ½ organic cucumber
– 100 g (4 oz) rocket /arugula
– 3 sprigs of mint
– flesh of 1 avocado
– 100 ml (³/₈ US / ²/₅ AU cup) coconut milk
– juice of 1 lime
– 150 ml (²/₃ US / ³/₅ AU cup) grapefruit juice
– 100 ml (³/₈ US / ²/₅ AU cup) mineral water
– ice cubes (optional)

Wash the cucumber, rocket and mint. Chop the cucumber coarsely. Blend the ingredients to a smooth purée using a regular blender or food processor or, failing that, you can use an immersion blender. If the smoothie is too thick for your liking, you can dilute it with a few ice cubes or with a little extra mineral water.

This is the power drink of my favourite business woman!

PEAR, PARSLEY AND LIME SMOOTHIE (100% RAW)

MAKES 2 GLASSES — PREPARATION 5 MINUTES

– 4 leaves of kale
– 1 bunch of flat leaf parsley
– 2 fully ripe pears
– 1 banana
– juice of ½ lime
– 250 ml (1 US / 1 AU cup) mineral water

_____

Wash the kale and the parsley. Peel and core the pears, peel the banana, then chop the fruit coarsely. Blend all of the ingredients to a smooth purée using a regular blender, food processor or a hand-held immersion blender. Add some ice cubes and drink the juice straight away.

NOTE

This smoothie is even better if the pear juice is extracted using a centrifugal juicer.

VARIATION

You can replace the parsley with dandelion greens.

This drink is popular with yoga lovers!

BLUEBERRY SMOOTHIE
MAKES 2 GLASSES – PREPARATION 5 MINUTES

– 250 g (8 ½ oz) blueberries
– 1 vanilla pod/bean
– 4 UK/US tbsp (3 AU tbsp) hemp seeds
– 2 egg whites
– 200 ml (⅞ US cup / ⅘ AU cup) almond milk (see page 226)
– 100 ml (⅜ US / ⅖ AU cup) mineral water

Wash the blueberries. Split the vanilla pod in two lengthways to extract the seeds. Put these in the bowl of a food processer or blender and add the remaining ingredients. Blend to a smooth purée and drink straight away, chilled with ice cubes if preferred.

NOTE
If you have a centrifugal juicer, use it to first extract the juice from the blueberries.

This is the ideal drink for chilling out creative types.

APPLEBERRY SMOOTHIE (100% RAW)

MAKES 2 GLASSES — PREPARATION 5 MINUTES

– 3 apples
– 50 g (2 oz) fresh or frozen cranberries
– 20 g (³/₄ oz) purslane or mâche/lamb's lettuce
– 3 sprigs of mint
– flesh of ¹/₂ avocado
– 150 ml (²/₃ US cup ³/₅ AU cup) mineral water

Wash the apples or peel them. If the cranberries are fresh, wash them, as well as the purslane and the mint. Pick the mint leaves off their stems. Remove the cores from the apples and chop the apples coarsely. Juice the apples, ideally using a centrifugal juicer, then add the cranberries. Pour the juice from the apples and cranberries into a blender or food processor, then add all of the other ingredients and blend to a purée. Drink straight away with or without ice.

NOTE

If you do not have a centrifugal juicer, put the ingredients progressively into a high-performance food processor or blender, and blend in stages to achieve a smooth loose mixture.

VARIATION

Purslane is a wild salad leaf and can be replaced by mâche (also known as 'lamb's lettuce') or by watercress or young spinach leaves. Instead of using whole cranberries, you can use approximately 5 tablespoons of pure cranberry juice.

MANGO, DATE AND PINEAPPLE SMOOTHIE

(100% RAW)

MAKES 2 GLASSES – PREPARATION 5 MINUTES

– a handful of rocket/arugula
– ¼ pineapple
– 1 vanilla pod/bean
– 1 mango
– juice of 1 lime
– 3 pitted dates
– 100 ml (³⁄₈ US / ²⁄₅ AU cup) mineral water

Wash the rocket and drain it. Cut away the skin and eyes from the quarter of pineapple and pass it through a centrifugal juicer. Split the vanilla pod in half and scrape out the seeds with the point of a knife. Peel the mango and cut away the flesh in chunks, discarding the stone. Put the vanilla seeds and mango flesh in the bowl of a food processor or blender. Add the pineapple juice, lime juice, the washed rocket, dates and mineral water. Blend to a smoothie and drink it straight away, with or without ice.

NOTE
The mango and the pineapple should be beautifully ripe so that they possess a natural sweetness. If you do not have a centrifugal juicer, put the ingredients progressively into a high-performance food processor or blender, and blend them in stages to achieve a smooth, evenly blended, purée.

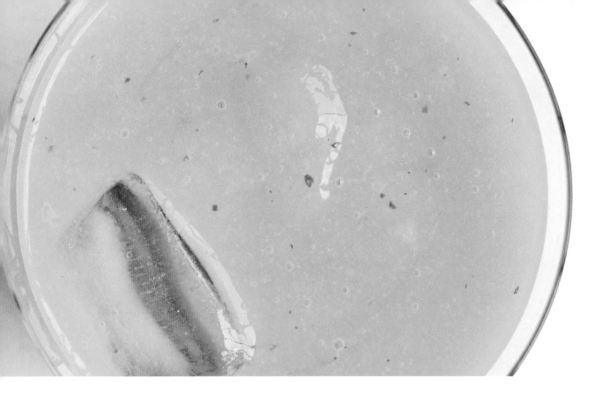

MANGO, ORANGE AND BASIL SMOOTHIE

MAKES 2 GLASSES — PREPARATION 5 MINUTES

100% RAW

- flesh of 2 mangos
- 8 washed basil leaves
- 250 ml (1 US/AU cup) organic orange juice

Use your preferred method of blending to blend the ingredients to a smoothie. Drink it immediately, adding a few ice-cubes, if you like, for a colder, fresher version.

NOTE

If you use a centrifugal juicer to extract the mango juice and fresh orange juice, the result will be even better. For 250 ml (1 US / AU cup) of orange juice, you will need 3 oranges.

I call this juice my 'little lift for kids in a state of collapse on the sofa'.

YELLOW COCONUT SMOOTHIE (100% RAW)

MAKES 2 GLASSES – PREPARATION 5 MINUTES

- flesh of ¼ pineapple
- flesh of ½ mango
- flesh of 1 peach
- 100 ml (³⁄₈ US / ²⁄₅ AU cup) coconut water

Use your preferred method of blending to blend the ingredients to a smoothie. Drink it straight away.

NOTE
Coconut water is found inside coconuts which are not fully ripe. Fortunately, it is also found in cartons and cans in most supermarkets and health-food stores.

If you have a centrifugal juicer to extract the juice from the fruit, the smoothie will be even better. If the drink is too thick for your liking, dilute it with a few ice-cubes.

CARROT AND ICE CREAM SMOOTHIE

MAKES 2 GLASSES — PREPARATION 5 MINUTES

– 150 ml (²/₃ US / ³/₅ AU cup) organic carrot juice
– 150 ml (²/₃ US / ³/₅ AU cup) organic apple juice
– 3 tsp maple syrup
– 2 scoops vanilla ice-cream

Choose only organic fruit juice of the highest quality. Use a blender or a food processor to blend the juice, along with the remaining ingredients, to a smoothie. Drink it straight away.

VARIATION

For a less sweet version, replace the vanilla ice cream with 150 ml (²/₃ US / ³/₅ AU cup) of home-made almond milk (see page 226).

NOTE

If you use vanilla ice cream made with rice milk instead of cow's milk, then this drink is a truly 'raw' drink.

If you have a centrifugal juicer, you can make the juices yourself using 5-6 carrots and 1 large juicy apple.

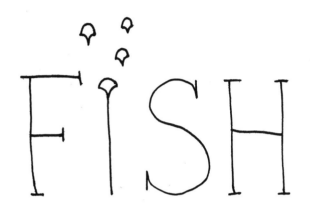

LEMON TUNA (100% RAW)

SERVES 4 – PREPARATION 15 MINUTES

CHILLING 1 HOUR

– 600 g (1 lb 5 oz) tuna fillet, lightly threaded with fat
– juice of 2 lemons
– 100 g (4 oz) white Chinese radish (daikon)
– 1/2 lemon confit
– 8 sprigs of fresh coriander leaves (cilantro)
– 2 tsp sesame oil
– 2 UK/US tbsp (1 1/2 AU tbsp) olive oil

- -

To make the sashimi, use a well-sharpened knife to slice the tuna into 1/2 –
1 cm (1/4 - 3/8 inch) thick rectangles, each about 4-5 cm (1 1/2 - 2 inches) long and
about 2 cm (3/4 inch) wide (see pages 16-17). Pour the lemon juice onto a tray or
flat plate that will accommodate the sashimi in a single layer. Lay the sashimi on
top so that one side can soak up the juice. Cover and transfer to the refrigerator
for 1 hour.

Trim and peel the radish. Use a peeling or grating tool, or small sharp paring
knife, to take long thin ribbons from the radish (see illustration, right). Chop
the lemon confit and discard the pips. Snip the coriander leaves. Put these 3
ingredients in a bowl and stir in the sesame and olive oil, turning the ingredients
to coat them evenly. Cover and chill.

Drain the sashimis and arrange them on a large serving plate. Distribute the
radish and lemon confit mixture on top of the sashimis and serve.

COCONUT AND PASSION FRUIT TUNA (100% RAW)

SERVES 6 — PREPARATION 20 MINUTES

FREEZING 1 HOUR

– 600 g (1 lb 5 oz) tuna fillet, lightly threaded with fat
– several spring onions/US scallions/AU shallots, depending on size
– 2 passion fruit
– 6 tsp coconut milk
– 3 tsp black sesame seeds
– sea salt and freshly ground pepper

_____

Put the tuna in the freezer for at least 1 hour.

Meanwhile, make the sauce. Slice the white part of the onion fairly thinly and chop the green tail; set aside. Cut the passion fruits in half. Use a small sharp spoon to scrape out the contents of each half into a small sieve set over a bowl. Press the pulp and pips with the spoon to extract as much juice as possible. Mix together the sieved juice, the coconut milk and the chopped onion. Season to taste with salt and freshly ground pepper. Set this sauce aside, chilled.

Use a well-sharpened knife – with a sufficiently long blade – to slice the tuna into slices 2 mm (about 1/8 inch) thick, (see pages 16-17). Arrange the slices on a large serving platter or on individual serving plates. Cover them with cling film (plastic wrap), and keep them chilled in the refrigerator.

Just before serving, drizzle over the reserved sauce and sprinkle with the black sesame seeds.

NOTE
The black sesame seeds can be found in health-food stores.

SWORDFISH, BASIL,
PINE NUTS AND TOMATOES
SERVES 6 – PREPARATION 10 MINUTES

– 600 g (1 lb 5 oz) swordfish
– 100 g (4 oz) drained tomato confit
– olive oil

FOR THE PESTO
– 100 ml ($^3/_8$ US / $^2/_5$ AU cup) olive oil
– 60 g (2 $^1/_2$ oz) petits pois/French baby peas
– 2 UK/US tbsp (1 $^1/_2$ AU tbsp) pine nuts
– $^1/_2$ bunch of basil
– sea salt and freshly ground pepper

_____

Rinse and pat dry the swordfish, then cut it into $^1/_2$ cm ($^1/_4$ inch) dice (see pages 16–17); transfer the fish to a bowl. Cut the tomato confits into small pieces, moisten them with a little olive oil then add them to the fish, stirring to distribute them evenly. Cover the bowl and set it aside in the refrigerator.

To make the pesto, pour the olive oil, petits pois, pine nuts and the basil leaves into the bowl of a food processor or blender. Add and salt and freshly ground pepper to taste. Pulse the mixture briefly, just enough to make the ingredients hold together, as illustrated.

Serve the tartare well-chilled, adding the sauce at the last moment.

VARIATION
For an even more 'raw food' version, you can replace the tomato confit with 50 g (2 oz) of dried tomatoes. Rehydrate the dried tomatoes before using them by steeping them in a mixture of 3 teaspoons of balsamic vinegar and lukewarm water for 1 hour.

RAW TUNA WITH VINAIGRETTE THÉRÈSE

SERVES 4 – PREPARATION 10 MINUTES

– 400 g (14 oz) tuna fillet, lightly threaded with fat
– about 4 cm (1 ½ inches) grated fresh ginger root
– juice of 1 lime
– 3 tsp strong mustard
– 3 tsp soy sauce
– 3 UK/US tbsp (2 AU tbsp plus a tsp) grape seed oil
– 1 lime, cut into quarters

Wash the fish, pat it dry, then cut it into bite-size pieces. Keep these morsels chilled in the refrigerator until you are ready to eat them.

Meanwhile, blend together the ginger, lime juice, mustard, soy sauce and grape seed oil to achieve a fairly thick vinaigrette which will serve as a dip. Transfer it to a small dish.

When you are ready, arrange the chilled tuna bites on a large serving platter and add the quarters of lime. Offer the vinaigrette separately. Serve the tuna and its vinaigrette dip with an aperitif among friends.

VARIATION
You can replace the grape seed oil with sunflower oil.

This dish brings back wonderful memories of Tahiti. Thank you, Thérèse, for your patience and willingness to share with us the secrets of this delicacy.

SCALLOPS WITH JERUSALEM ARTICHOKES AND VANILLA (100% RAW)

SERVES 6 — PREPARATION 15 MINUTES

– 20 very fresh scallops, without coral
– 4 small and firm Jerusalem artichokes
– 2 vanilla pods/beans
– 4 UK/US tbsp (3 AU tbsp) olive oil
– 3 tsp chopped hazelnuts
– 2 sprigs of chervil
– 4 UK/US tbsp (3 AU tbsp) olive oil
– sea salt and freshly ground pepper

- -

Split the vanilla pods in two lengthways and scrape out the seeds into a bowl using a small knife. Add the olive oil, stirring to mix, then set this vanilla-flavoured oil aside.

Rinse the scallops, pat them dry, cut them into small even-sized morsels then put them in a mixing bowl. Peel the Jerusalem artichokes, cut them into small cubes and add them to the bowl, along with the chopped hazelnuts and sprigs of chervil, snipped or coarsely chopped. Gently turn the ingredients to distribute them, then stir in the flavoured oil and turn them again to coat evenly. Add freshly ground pepper. Taste and add salt as desired. Cover and chill the mixture until you are ready to enjoy it.

LANGOUSTINES WITH
ESPELETTE PEPPER (100% RAW)

SERVES 4 – PREPARATION 20 MINUTES

– 16 very fresh langoustines/Dublin Bay prawns/US crayfish/AU scampi
– 3 UK/US tbsp (2 AU tbsp plus 1 tsp) olive oil
– juice and zest of 1 organic lime
– sea salt
– 2 pinches of Espelette pepper
– coriander/cilantro flowers, or herbs of your choice (optional)

_____

To prepare the langoustines, pull off the head and legs, then peel away the shell. With a small, sharp knife, make a slit down the centre of the curved back of each langoustine and remove the bitter-tasting black intestinal vein with the point of the knife. Rinse the langoustines and dry gently with kitchen paper. Put them on a large plate, cover with cling film (plastic wrap) and keep them chilled until the moment of eating.

Meanwhile, prepare the seasoning: mix together the olive, lime juice, a little sea salt and the Espelette pepper; set aside. Just before serving, stir the seasoning and pour it over the langoustines. Scatter with the lime zest and some coriander flowers or a few fresh herbs of your choice. Serve without delay.

NOTE

Espelette pepper is cultivated from chilli peppers in the small village of Espelette in the French Basque region. It is prized for its non-aggressive smokey flavour and has become popular with chefs all over the world. If you cannot obtain it, you can substitute either a very mild chilli pepper (so not cayenne) or black pepper.

Make sure your fishmonger sells you only the freshest langoustines – alive is even better!

SEABASS WITH GINGER AND RADISH (100% RAW)

SERVES 6 — PREPARATION 20 MINUTES

MARINATING 6 HOURS OR OVERNIGHT

– 600 g (1 lb 5 oz) fillet of seabass
– 3 UK/US tbsp (2 AU tbsp plus 1 tsp) grated fresh ginger root
– 50 – 100 ml (1/5 – 2/5 US / AU cup) olive oil
– a good bunch of radish of various colours
– coriander/cilantro flowers (optional)
– sea salt and freshly ground pepper

Rinse the seabass and pat it dry. Line the bottom of a large serving plate with half of the grated ginger. Arrange the fillets of fish on top then sprinkle with the remaining half of the ginger. Drizzle the fish with enough olive oil to moisten it evenly then cover the plate with cling film (plastic wrap). Transfer it to the refrigerator and leave the fish to marinate for at least 6 hours and up to 12 hours.

To complete the tartare, wash the radishes well and trim them. If you like, you can keep the stalks to make a soup. Cut the radishes into small cubes and put them in a mixing bowl. Wipe the marinated fish, guarding the oil in which it was steeped. Use a well-sharpened knife to cut the fillets of fish into small even-sized morsels (see pages 16-17). Combine the pieces of fish with the radish. Strain the oil through a fine sieve set over a jug and set it aside. Unless you are ready to serve the tartare immediately, cover it and keep it chilled.

Just before serving, arrange the tartare on individual serving plates. Drizzle the strained oil on top and season to taste with salt and freshly ground pepper. Serve without delay.

NOTE
Check with your fishmonger that the seabass is sufficiently fresh to be eaten raw.

If you cannot find multi-coloured radish, use traditional red radish.

SCALLOPS WITH PARMESAN AND PEPPER

SERVES 4 – PREPARATION 15 MINUTES

CHILLING 1 HOUR

- 12 scallops
- 1 tsp chilli oil
- 2 UK/US tbsp (1 ½ AU tbsp) olive oil
- 20 g (³⁄₄ oz) Parmesan
- 2 or 3 chives
- zest of 1 organic lime
- fleur de sel and freshly ground pepper

Rinse the scallops and pat them dry. Remove any remaining coral. Arrange the scallops on a freezer-proof plate, cover with cling film (plastic wrap) and transfer to the freezer for 1 hour.

Use a well-sharpened knife to slice horizontally through each scallop to yield 3 or 4 very thin slices; arrange these on a flat plate. If you are not ready to serve the scallops straight away, you can keep them covered and chilled in the refrigerator for up to several hours but no longer.

Mix together the 2 types of oil and, when you are ready to serve the scallops, drizzle the oil gently on top. With a small sharp knife or peel, make shavings from the Parmesan and scatter them over the surface. Snip the chives and sprinkle them on top along with the zest of lime. Add salt and pepper to taste and serve without delay.

VARIATION

For a more luxurious version, you can replace the oils used here with truffle-scented oil. If you do this, it is important to omit the lime zest.

CEVICHE OF WHITE FISH (100% RAW)

SERVES 4 – PREPARATION 20 MINUTES

CHILLING 1^1/$_2$ - 2 HOURS

– 400 g (14 oz) white firm-fleshed fish fillets
– ^{1}/$_2$ red chilli pepper
– 1 small, sweet or mild-tasting onion
– juice and zest of 2 organic limes
– ^{1}/$_2$ tsp soft light brown sugar/raw caster

– 10 sprigs of coriander/cilantro
– 4 sprigs of flat leaf parsley
– 10 cherry tomatoes
– olive oil
– salt and freshly ground pepper

In France we use the strictly Mediterranean fish, rascasse. However, it can be replaced with any white firm-fleshed fish. Options include dogfish, swordfish, catfish, thick fillet of cod, gurnard, halibut, bream and seabass.

To make a marinade for the fish, start by preparing the chilli. Wearing gloves to protect your hands, split the chilli in half, scrape away the seeds, and slice or dice the chilli very finely. (If you handle the chilli without protecting your skin, be sure to wash your hands well afterwards). Peel and thinly slice the onion. In a bowl, mix the lime juice with the sugar, stirring to dissolve the sugar. Mix in the chilli and the onion. Chop or snip the leaves of coriander and parsley and stir half of them into the marinade, setting the remainder aside in an airtight container.

Wash the fish and cut it into thin slices, or small nuggets or cubes, according to your taste. Put the fish on a plate with a shallow bowl and pour over the marinade. Cover with cling film (or plastic wrap) and transfer the fish to a refrigerator to marinate for about 1^1/$_2$ hours depending on personal preferences – the longer the fish marinates the more 'cooked' it will become. However, it generally risks falling apart after 2 hours.

Meanwhile, wash the tomatoes, cut them in half, discard the pips and chop them into small pieces.

Just before serving, garnish the ceviche with the morsels of tomato. Add a drizzle of oil. Taste, and season the ceviche lightly. Scatter over the remaining herbs and the zest of lime then serve without delay.

RAW FISH WITH COCONUT (100% RAW)

SERVES 4 – PREPARATION 40 MINUTES

– 400 g (14 oz) firm-fleshed fish fillets*
– about 4 bulbs and 2 stems of spring onions/US scallions/AU shallots
– ½ cucumber
– 2 coconuts
– juice of 3 limes
– salt and freshly ground pepper

Options for the firm-fleshed fish include tuna, cod, sea bream, halibut, sea bass and Pollack.

Wash the fish, pat it dry and cut it into cubes; cover and chill. Trim and finely slice the white bulb part of the spring onions and cut one of the green stems into about 8 sections. Peel the cucumber, cut it in half lengthways, remove the seeds, then slice or dice it. Break open the coconuts, remove the flesh and grate it.

To extract coconut milk from the grated flesh, use a centrifugal juicer if you have one. Alternatively, place the flesh in the centre of a clean tea towel (dish towel). Gather the corners of the towel and twist them to form a ball. Working over a bowl, tighten the twisted towel several times to squeeze out milk from the coconut flesh. This may seem a tedious job but it produces coconut milk that is so much better than the bought versions.

In a bowl, mix together the reserved fish, the coconut milk, the spring onion and shallot, and the cucumber. Cover and chill for at least 1 hour. Immediately before serving, stir in the lime juice and season lightly with salt and pepper.

VARIATION

For a 'hot' version of this dish, add a small red chilli pepper which you have deseeded and chopped or sliced very finely. For a 'lazy' version, replace the freshly extracted coconut milk with 150 ml (⅔ US / ⅗ AU cup) of commercial coconut milk.

Once again, a dish which takes me back to Tahiti and aperitif time!

THOMAS BENADY – LA MACHINE
À COUDES

I adore this little bistro, worthy of being a grand restaurant! Thomas plays with natural flavours in the kitchen while the beautiful Marlène sparkles in the dining room.

– – – – – – – – – – – – – – –

LA MACHINE À COUDES
35 Rue Nationale
92100 Boulogne

MARINATED MACKEREL

SERVES 4 – PREPARATION 30 MINUTES
MARINATING 24 HOURS + 2 HOURS

– 4 fillets of Atlantic mackerel / AU yellowtail horse mackerel, skin intact
– 6 sprigs of coriander/cilantro
– fleur de sel

FOR THE MARINADE FOR THE FISH
– 100 ml ($^3/_8$ US / $^2/_5$ AU cup) grape seed oil
– zest of 1 lemon
– the grated rind of 1 kaffir lime

FOR THE CUCUMBER AND ITS MARINADE
– 3 small cucumbers
– 5 UK/US tbsp (4 AU tbsp plus 1 tsp) caster/superfine sugar
– 100 ml ($^3/_8$ US / $^2/_5$ AU cup) water
– 100 ml ($^3/_8$ US / $^2/_5$ AU cup) white wine vinegar

FOR THE TABOULEH OF CAULIFLOWER
– $^1/_2$ cauliflower
– 1 $^1/_2$ rinsed lemon confit
– 4 UK/US tbsp (3 AU tbsp) fruity olive oil
– 1 tsp Espelette pepper or other mild chilli pepper
– 1 tsp fine salt
– juice of 1 lemon (added at the moment of serving)

FOR THE REDCURRANT SAUCE
– 125 g (about $^3/_4$ US/AU cup) redcurrants
– juice of $^1/_2$ lemon
– 2 tsp caster/superfine sugar
– 2 UK/US tbsp (1 $^1/_2$ AU tbsp) water

– –

The night before you serve the dish, combine the marinade ingredients for the fish in a small bowl. Cover and chill in the refrigerator for 24 hours. On the day, wash the fillets of mackerel, pat them dry and arrange them side by side on a flat plate. Spoon over the marinade, distributing it evenly. Cover with cling film (plastic wrap) then transfer to the refrigerator for at least 2 hours.

Wash the cucumbers, retaining their skin. Cut them in 4 lengthways, then put the quarters in a large jar. Mix together the sugar, water and vinegar for the cucumbers marinade then pour it into the jar. Close the jar and refrigerate it for 1-2 hours. Wash and dry the cauliflower then divide it into florets. Use a peeler, or a small sharp knife, to reduce the florets to large crumbs resembling a coarse semolina. Transfer the crumbs into a bowl. Dice the lemon confit and add it to the bowl along with the olive oil, Espelette pepper and salt to taste. Mix well, cover and set aside.

To make the redcurrant sauce, use your preferred blending tool to blend the ingredients to a smooth purée.

Just before serving, drain the fillets of fish and the cucumbers; discard the marinating liquids. Distribute 1 fillet to each serving plate. Chop or snip the coriander and use about half of it to garnish the fish. Arrange 3 pieces of cucumber decoratively on top. Stir the juice of half a lemon into the tabouleh to complete it, then add the remaining half of coriander. Distribute 2 heaped tablespoons of tabouleh and a few little pools of redcurrant sauce to each plate. If you like, garnish with a slice of raw red beetroot. Sprinkle with fleur de sel and serve straight away.

RAW MACKEREL IN COCONUT MILK (100% RAW)

SERVES 6 – PREPARATION 15 MINUTES
MARINATING 6 HOURS

– 6 very fresh fillets of mackerel, with skin intact
– 150 ml (²/₃ US /³/₅ AU cup) coconut milk
– juice of 1 lime
– 6 cherry tomatoes
– ¹/₂ red chilli pepper (optional)
– 6 sprigs of coriander/cilantro
– a few snipped chives
– 6 wedges of lime
– salt and freshly ground pepper

Wash the fillets of mackerel, pat them dry and remove any small remaining bones that may have been left behind by the fishmonger. Cut the fillets lengthways into thin slices and arrange them side by side in a large dish that will accommodate marinating liquid.

For the marinade, mix together the coconut milk and lime juice, then season to taste with salt and pepper. Pour half of this marinade over the fish, reserving the remainder. Cover the fish with cling film (plastic wrap) and put it in the refrigerator for 6 hours.

Meanwhile, wash the tomatoes, cut them in half, discard the pips and any bits of core. Chop them into small pieces and add them to the remaining half of the marinating mixture to make an accompanying sauce. If you are adding some chilli pepper, wear gloves to protect your hands, then split the chilli in half and scrape away the seeds. Dice it finely and add it to the coconut and tomato sauce.

To serve, drain the fillets and transfer them to individual plates. Drizzle over the coconut and tomato sauce. Chop or snip the coriander leaves and chives, then sprinkle the mixture on top. Garnish each plate with a wedge of lime and serve.

NOTE
Ask your fishmonger to fillet the mackerel for you, leaving the skin intact. You can also ask him to remove as many of the smaller bones as possible.

TARTARE OF YELLOW POLLOCK WITH CHORIZO

SERVES 4 – PREPARATION 20 MINUTES

– 400 g (14 oz) very fresh yellow Pollock, coley, cod or whiting
– about 5 spring onions/US scallions/AU shallots
– 2 slices of chorizo sausage about ½ cm (¼ inch) thick, weighing 20 g (¾ oz)
– 25 g (1 oz) petits pois/French baby peas
– 2 sprigs of tarragon
– 50 g (2 oz) sprouting lentils (optional)
– 3 UK/US tbsp (2 AU tbsp plus 1 tsp) olive oil
– salt and freshly ground pepper

_____

Wash the fish, pat it dry, then cut it into small cubes. Trim and finely slice the white bulb part of the spring onions and cut 1 or 2 of the green stems into about 8 sections. You can use more or less of the green stem section depending on your personal taste.

Chop the chorizo sausage into very small dice. Transfer these ingredients to a mixing bowl.

Either crush the peas with a fork, or blend them very briefly without letting them form a purée. Snip the tarragon leaves. Add the peas and leaves to the bowl, along with the sprouting lentils. Turn the mixture to distribute ingredients evenly, drizzling over the olive oil and seasoning to taste lightly with salt. Eat the dish straight away – it is good to eat without necessarily being chilled.

OYSTERS MARINATED IN LIME JUICE (100% RAW)

FOR 12 OYSTERS – PREPARATION 15 MINUTES
MARINATING 1 HOUR

– 12 oysters, ideally small, no. 3 size, and rinsed in fresh water
– juice and zest of $1/2$ organic lime
– 3 tsp olive oil
– 3 sprigs of snipped or chopped coriander/cilantro
– freshly ground pepper

- -

To make the marinade, use a dish or a plate with a shallow bowl that is large enough to accommodate the oysters when removed from their shells. Mix together the lime juice and zest with the olive oil, then stir in the coriander; set aside briefly.

To open the oysters, take each one and hold it in a cloth, with the flatter shell upwards. Insert the tip of an oyster knife into the hinge and twist it to open the shells. Discard any liquid which escapes. Slide the knife along the inside of the upper shell to cut the muscle that attaches it to the flesh. Pull off the upper shell. Slide the knife under the oyster to detach it from its lower shell and gently slide the oyster, along with its juices, into the marinade. Repeat with the remaining oysters, reserving their lower shells. Turn the oysters in the marinade to coat them evenly. Cover the dish with cling film (plastic wrap) and transfer it to the refrigerator for 1 hour, turning the oysters over after 30 minutes.

When you are ready to serve the oysters, transfer them to their lower shells and arrange them on a serving plate. Add a turn of the pepper mill and serve straight away.

TIP
I prepare the marinade in advance and combine it with the oysters about 1 hour before I want to serve aperitifs.

JOHN DORY WITH LIQUORICE-INFUSED OIL (100% RAW)

SERVES 4 – PREPARATION 15 MINUTES

MARINATING 6 HOURS

- 200 g (7 oz) fillets of John Dory, or fillets of bream, sole, turbot or sea bass
- 2 UK/US tbsp (1 ½ AU tbsp) olive oil
- 2 UK/US tbsp (1 ½ AU tbsp) hazelnut oil or pumpkin seed oil
- 1 large sliver of fresh liquorice root
- 1 handful of young beetroot (salad) leaves, or other small salad leaves of your choice
- fleur de sel

Wash and pat dry the fillets of fish and arrange them in a single layer on a large plate or dish with a shallow bowl. Coat the fillets with the 2 types of oil and finely grate about half of the liquorice root on top, reserving the remainder. Cover the plate with cling film (plastic wrap) and transfer it to the refrigerator. After 3 hours, turn over the fillets of fish and finely grate the remaining liquorice root over the surface. Cover again and leave the fish to marinate in the refrigerator for a further 3 hours.

Slice the fish into small even-sized nuggets and arrange them on serving plates. Drizzle over most of the marinating liquid in a fine stream. Use the last of the marinade to dress the salad leaves; arrange these on the plates. Sprinkle with fleur de sel and serve without delay.

NOTE

Ask your fishmonger for the freshest possible fish and make sure he knows that it is going to be eaten raw.

Fresh liquorice root can be found in health-food stores and, sometimes, in pharmacies. When you grate it, use a very fine disc.

CEVICHE OF LOBSTER WITH LIME (100% RAW)

SERVES 4 — PREPARATION 25 MINUTES

FREEZING 2 HOURS

CHILLING ABOUT 2 HOURS

– 2 uncooked, shelled lobster tails
– 3-4 spring onions/US scallions/AU shallots
– 20 g (3/4 oz) sweet red pepper
– zest of 1 lime
– a small handful of watercress leaves (optional)

FOR THE MARINADE
– 3 tsp chopped dulse seaweed

– 3 UK/US tbsp (2 AU tbsp plus 1 tsp) lime juice, or Japanese yuzu juice
– 1 tsp organic soy sauce
– 3 tsp rice vinegar
– 2 UK/US tbsp (1 1/2 AU tbsp) sunflower oil
– a pinch of Espelette pepper or other mild chilli pepper

Wrap the shelled lobster tails in cling film (plastic wrap) and put them in the freezer for 2 hours.

Meanwhile, prepare the marinade. Combine all of the ingredients for the marinade in a mixing bowl, stirring well to blend them. Cover and reserve in a cool place or in the refrigerator.

When the lobster is almost ready to come out of the freezer, trim the spring onions. Trim the onions and chop the white bulbs into tiny dice. Cut a couple of the green stems into strips or pieces to suit personal taste. Scrape away any remaining seeds from the red pepper then chop it into tiny dice of a similar size to the onion.

Remove the wrapping from the lobster. Use a well-sharpened knife to slice the tails as thinly as possible. Arrange the slices on serving plates. Spoon over the reserved marinade and scatter the chopped onion and pepper on top, along with the lime zest. Cover each plate with cling film (plastic wrap) and put them in the refrigerator for up to 2 hours, depending on how 'cooked' you like your ceviche to be.

Serve the ceviche well chilled. Watercress leaves make a lovely garnish but if you do not have them, you can add a few fresh herbs of your choice.

NOTE
For the lobster tails, ask your fishmonger to remove the shells and discard the intestines.

Dulse seaweed and Japanese yuzu juice (which tastes like a cross between grapefruit and lemon juice) can be found in Asian grocers, health-food stores and online.

CARPACCIO OF BEEF TRADITIONAL STYLE

SERVES 4 – PREPARATION 15 MINUTES
FREEZING 2 HOURS

– 400 g (14 oz) fillet or
  tenderloin of beef
– 40 g (1 ½ oz) freshly grated
  Parmesan shavings
– 4 sprigs of basil

FOR THE SAUCE
– juice of 1 lemon
– 4 UK/US tbsp (3 AU tbsp)
  olive oil
– fleur de sel and freshly
  ground pepper

Wrap the beef in cling film (plastic wrap) and put it in the freezer for 2 hours. Meanwhile, make a vinaigrette sauce by whisking together the lemon juice with the olive oil, then adding salt and pepper to taste. Set aside.

When the beef is sufficiently frozen, remove it from the freezer and take off the wrapping. Have ready 4 chilled serving plates. Using a well-sharpened knife, cut the beef into very thin, almost translucent slices, arranging them neatly on the plates as you proceed. Drizzle the reserved sauce over the sliced beef. Use a peeler or a small sharp knife to make shavings of Parmesan and scatter these on top, along with some basil leaves. Add a turn of the pepper mill and serve immediately.

CARPACCIO OF BEEF REVISITED

SERVES 4 – PREPARATION 20 MINUTES
FREEZING 2 HOURS

– 400 g (14 oz) fillet or
  tenderloin of beef
– 10 small white button
  mushrooms
– 4 asparagus spears
– about 6 bulbs and 2 stems of
  spring onions/US scallions
  AU shallots
– 4 pitted black olives
– 50 ml (¼ US/ ⅕ AU cup)
  olive oil
– fleur de sel and freshly
  ground pepper

Wrap the beef in cling film (plastic wrap) and put it in the freezer for 2 hours.

Meanwhile, wipe the mushrooms with a damp cloth. Peel away any tough woody skin from the asparagus spears and cut the stalk sections into thin rounds; reserve the tips separately. Slice the white bulbs and green stems of the spring onions very thinly. If you like, you can include a couple of extra stems, sliced into long strips. Set these vegetables aside. For the sauce, put the asparagus tips and the olives into the bowl of a food processor or blender. Add the olive oil and a little salt and pepper. Pulse the mixture several times very briefly. Set the sauce aside.

When the beef is sufficiently frozen, remove it from the freezer and take off the wrapping. Have ready 4 chilled serving plates. Using a well-sharpened knife, cut the beef into very thin, almost translucent slices, arranging them neatly on the plates as you proceed. Drizzle the reserved sauce over the sliced beef. Distribute the prepared asparagus and onions on top. At the last moment, slice the mushrooms very thinly, preferably using a mandoline. Scatter a few slices over each assembly and serve straight away.

DRIED BEEF,
PEAR AND CAULIFLOWER

SERVES 4 – PREPARATION 20 MINUTES

– 200 g (7 oz) dried bresaola beef, sliced thinly into about 32 slices
– 6 cauliflower florets
– 2 ripe small seasonal pears
– juice of 1 lemon
– 2 UK/US tbsp (1 ½ AU tbsp) coarsely chopped walnuts
– small tarragon leaves, plucked from several sprigs

FOR THE DRESSING
– 3 tsp maple syrup
– 2 UK/US tbsp (1 ½ AU tbsp) hazelnut oil
– 2 UK/US tbsp (1 ½ AU tbsp) olive oil
– fleur de sel and freshly ground pepper

Wash and dry the cauliflower florets; use a grater or peeler to reduce the florets to large, coarse crumbs resembling semolina. Set aside. You can peel the pears or not, just as you wish. Cut them into quarters and core them. Cut each quarter into thin slices, drizzling them with lemon juice as you work to prevent them from turning brown.

On serving plates, alternate slices of beef and pear. Sprinkle with the reserved cauliflower semolina, coarsely chopped walnuts and tarragon leaves. Make a dressing by whisking together the maple syrup with the oils and a little salt and pepper. Drizzle the dressing at the last moment.

MY GRAVLAX OF BEEF

SERVES 6-8 — PREPARATION 15 MINUTES
CHILLING 24 HOURS

- 800 g (1 lb 12 oz) fillet or tenderloin of beef
- 1 shallot/AU eschallot
- juice and zest of 1 organic lime
- about 4 UK/US tbsp (3 AU tbsp) soft light brown sugar raw caster
- about 2 UK/US tbsp (1 1/2 AU tbsp) coarse sea salt
- about 3-4 UK/US tbsp (3 AU tbsp) organic soy sauce
- 3 tsp fennel seeds
- 3cm (1 1/4 inches) long, grated fresh ginger root
- 1 dried red bird's eye chilli pepper
- 1 sprig of Thai basil (optional)
- 3 sprigs of coriander/cilantro
- 2 sprigs of mint
- 3 tsp olive oil
- 3 sprigs of dill
- fleur de sel and freshly ground pepper

Select a dish large enough to accommodate the beef and its marinating mixture. Finely chop the shallot and distribute over the bottom of the dish. Add the juice and zest of lime, the sugar, salt, soy sauce, fennel seeds and grated ginger. Crush the dried red bird's eye chilli pepper, discarding the seeds; scatter it on top. Chop or snip all of the herbs, except for a sprig of dill for the garnish. Add the chopped herbs to the marinating mixture. Drizzle over the olive oil.

Put the fillet of beef in the dish and turn the meat to coat it evenly. Taste the marinade and adjust seasoning and sugar to taste. Cover the dish with cling film (plastic wrap) and transfer it to the refrigerator for 24 hours, turning the meat occasionally in its marinade.

When the beef has marinated sufficiently, wipe it lightly and transfer it to a carving board. Cut the meat into fairly thin slices, according to taste, and transfer them to a serving platter or to individual plates. Snip the remaining sprig of dill and scatter it over the beef. Adjust seasoning with a little salt and pepper. Serve immediately.

RAW BEEF MARINATED IN PEPPER

SERVES 4-8 – PREPARATION 25 MINUTES
CHILLING 24 HOURS

- 400 g (14 oz) fillet or
  tenderloin of beef
- 3 tsp green peppercorns
- 3 tsp Sichuan/Szechuan
  peppercorns
- 3 tsp white peppercorns
- 3 tsp black peppercorns
- a small amount of olive oil
- smoked salt

Slice the fillet of beef into 4 equal pieces. Crush with a mortar and pestle or very coarsely grind all the peppercorns and spread the mixture on a large plate. Brush the pieces of beef with the olive oil, then roll the beef in the pepper mixture. Wrap each piece of beef in cling film (plastic wrap) and chill in the refrigerator for at least 24 hours.

Remove the chilled beef from the refrigerator, and unwrap it. Using a brush or the edge of a spoon, remove the pepper from the beef. With a well-sharpened knife, cut the beef into thin slices and arrange them on serving plates. Sprinkle smoked salt on top.

Serve immediately either as a first course or appetizer.

VARIATION
Serve the marinated beef with a few leaves of well-seasoned rocket (arugula), avocado mayonnaise (see page 214) or even a dash of lemon juice.

VEAL AND PESTO CARPACCIO

SERVES 4 – PREPARATION 25 MINUTES

FREEZING 2 HOURS

– 400 g (14 oz) round of veal, from the upper-hind leg
– 1 lemon

FOR THE PESTO
– 1 peeled and chopped garlic clove, green germ removed
– 1 large bunch of basil
– 2 UK/US tbsp (1 1/2 AU tbsp) pine nuts
– 50 g (2 oz / 1/4 US/AU cup) freshly grated shavings of Parmesan
– 150 ml (2/3 US / 3/5 AU cup) olive oil
– freshly ground pepper

Wrap the round of veal in cling film (plastic wrap) and put it in the freezer for at least 2 hours. When the veal is sufficiently frozen, remove it from the freezer and take off the wrapping. Have ready 4 chilled serving plates. Using a well-sharpened knife, cut the veal into very thin, almost translucent slices, arranging them neatly on the plates as you proceed. Cover the plates in cling film (plastic wrap) and place them in the refrigerator until needed.

To make the pesto, put the garlic, basil leaves, pine nuts, Parmesan shavings, olive oil and a little pepper into the bowl of a food processor or blender. Blend the ingredients to obtain a smooth mixture.

Remove the plates of veal from the refrigerator and unwrap them. Cut the lemon into quarters, adding a section to each plate. Drizzle over the pesto and serve straight away.

VARIATION
For extra garnish, add a large bunch of seasoned rocket (arugula) to the carpaccio. You can also replace the veal with beef.

NOTE
If your butcher is friendly, don't hesitate to ask him for help in freezing and slicing the carpaccio. He will probably have the ideal slicing machine. Otherwise, it's up to you!

RAW TALENT   KAORI ENDO - NANASHI
☆☆☆   Kaori certainly thinks 'green'! She blends
             nature and lifestyle together in her Bento
             boxes with a wild talent.

NANASHI
57 rue Charlot   31 rue de Paradis
75003   75010 Paris

TARTARE OF DUCK JAPANESE STYLE

SERVES 4 – PREPARATION 20 MINUTES

MARINATING 1 HOUR

– 1 skinless duck breast
– 1 ripe Japanese persimmon fruit/kaki
– 1 Jerusalem artichoke/helianthi
– 2 florets of Romanesco or cauliflower
– 4 egg yolks
– 6 sprigs of coriander/cilantro
– 3 tsp roasted and crushed hazelnuts

– 2 UK/US tbsp (1 ½ AU tbsp) miso soup powder
– 1 small, peeled and grated garlic clove
– 1 cm (³/8 inch) long, peeled and grated
  ginger root
– 2 UK/US tbsp (1 ½ AU tbsp) sesame oil

FOR THE MARINADE
– 1 small green chilli pepper
– 1 lime
– 3 tsp organic whole cane sugar/radapura

Wash and dry the vegetables, herbs and fruit. To make the marinade, split the green chilli pepper and remove the seeds. Dice it finely and set aside. With a zester, scrape fine, pith-free zests from half of the lime. Squeeze the lime for its juice and put this in a mixing bowl (large enough to accommodate the duck) along with the zest. Stir in the sugar, miso powder, garlic, ginger and sesame oil. To complete the marinade, add enough of the chopped chilli pepper to suit your taste.

For the tartare, cut the duck breast into dice of about ½ cm (¼ inch) and add them to the marinade, turning to coat the meat evenly. Cover and transfer to the refrigerator for one hour.

Meanwhile, prepare a garnish: peel the persimmon and dice the flesh finely. Peel the Jerusalem artichoke and, with a mandoline or sharp knife, cut it into wafer-thin slices. Slice the florets of Romanesco equally finely. Snip the coriander leaves.

Distribute the marinated tartare between 4 serving plates and put an egg yolk in the centre of each. Sprinkle with the coriander and hazelnuts then scatter with the diced persimmon and vegetable garnish.

VEAL CARPACCIO 1

SERVES 4 – PREPARATION 25 MINUTES
FREEZING 2 HOURS

– 400 g (14 oz) round of veal,
  from the upper-hind leg
– 12 pitted Niçoise or Kalamata
  olives, or the black olives of
  your choice
– 3-4 spring onions/US
  scallions/AU shallots
– 8 pink radishes
– sea salt and freshly
  ground pepper

FOR THE DRESSING
– 4 UK/US tbsp (3 AU tbsp)
  olive oil
– 3 tsp maple syrup
– 1 tsp green Tabasco sauce

Wrap the round of veal in cling film (plastic wrap) and put it in the freezer for at least 2 hours. When the veal is sufficiently frozen, remove it from the freezer and take off the wrapping. Have ready 4 chilled serving plates. Using a well-sharpened knife, cut the veal into very thin, almost translucent, slices, arranging them neatly on the plates as you proceed. Slice the olives in thirds lengthways. Slice the white bulbs and a couple of the green stems of the onions very thinly. Slice the radishes into paper-thin slices. Distribute the olives, onions and radishes evenly over the veal. Cover the plates in cling film (plastic wrap) and place them in the refrigerator while you make the dressing.

For the dressing, whisk together the olive oil, maple syrup and green Tabasco sauce. Remove the plates of veal from the refrigerator and unwrap them. Drizzle the dressing over the sliced veal. Sprinkle a little salt on top and finish with one turn of the peppermill. Serve straight away.

VEAL CARPACCIO 2

SERVES 4 – PREPARATION 30 MINUTES
FREEZING 2 HOURS

- 400 g (14 oz) round of veal
  from the upper-hind leg
- a handful of washed
  bean sprouts
- the chopped leaves from 4
  sprigs of coriander/cilantro
- 3 tsp sesame seeds
- the zest of 1 organic lemon
- fleur de sel and freshly
  ground pepper

FOR THE DRESSING
- 4 UK/US tbsp (3 AU tbsp)
  organic soy sauce
- 1 tsp maple syrup
- 1 tsp sesame seed oil
- 1 trimmed and chopped fresh
  lemongrass stalk
- about 3 cm (1 1/4 inches) grated
  fresh ginger root

Wrap the veal in cling film (plastic wrap) and put it in the freezer for at least 2 hours. When the veal is sufficiently frozen, remove it from the freezer and take off the wrapping. Have ready 4 chilled serving plates. Using a well-sharpened knife, cut the veal into very thin, almost translucent slices, arranging them neatly on the plates as you proceed. Cover the plates with cling film (plastic wrap) and put them in the refrigerator until you are almost ready to serve.

Make the dressing in a small bowl, whisking together the soy sauce, maple syrup and sesame seed oil. Stir in the chopped lemongrass and grated ginger root.

Just before serving, remove the plates of veal from the refrigerator and unwrap them. Drizzle the dressing over the sliced veal. Distribute the bean sprouts, chopped coriander, sesame seeds and lemon zest on top. Add one turn of the peppermill and a little salt to each plate. Serve straight away.

VEAL TARTARE WITH OYSTERS AND SEAWEED

SERVES 4 — PREPARATION 15 MINUTES

– 10 oysters, ideally no. 2, medium-size, rinsed in fresh water
– 400 g (14 oz) fillet or tenderloin of veal
– 1 fat-bulbed new onion with green stem (or substitute a shallot/AU eschallot)
– a good pinch of dried seaweed
– 2 sprigs of flat leaf parsley
– about 8 small chives
– a small amount of wasabi
– 3 tsp hazelnut oil
– 2 UK/US tbsp (1 ½ AU tbsp) olive oil
– sea salt and freshly ground pepper

To open the oysters, take each one and hold it in a cloth, with the flatter shell upwards. Working over a small bowl to catch the oyster juice, insert the tip of an oyster knife into the hinge and twist it to open the shell. Slide the knife along the inside of the upper shell to cut the muscle that attaches it to the flesh. Pull off the upper shell, catching the juices in the small bowl. Cover and reserve this oyster juice. Slide the knife under the oyster to detach it then gently slide it on to a chopping board. Chop the oysters into small bite-size pieces and put them in a fairly large mixing bowl.

To complete the tartare mixture, cut the veal into ½ cm (¼ inch) dice and combine the diced veal with the oysters. Finely slice the onion, or shallot. Chop the seaweed and the parsley. Snip the chives into sections. Add all of these ingredients to the mixing bowl. Toss the tartare to distribute the ingredients evenly. Cover the bowl with cling film (plastic wrap) and transfer it to the refrigerator until it is well-chilled.

Meanwhile, mix the wasabi with the oyster juice and the 2 types of oil. Taste, and adjust seasoning with salt and pepper.

To serve, stir the wasabi dressing into the tartare. Adjust seasoning if necessary. Arrange the tartare, well-chilled, on individual plates and serve without delay.

THAI TARTARE

SERVES 4 – PREPARATION 25 MINUTES

– 600 g (1 lb 5 oz) fillet or tenderloin of beef
– 2 small red chilli peppers
– about 8 spring onions/US scallions/AU shallots
– about 4 cm (1 ½ inches) fresh ginger root
– a handful of Thai basil leaves (optional)
– a handful of coriander/cilantro leaves
– 2 lemongrass stalks, tough base and outer
  leaves discarded

FOR THE DRESSING
– 4 UK/US tbsp (3 AU tbsp) olive oil
– 4 tsp nuoc cham sauce
– 2 organic limes

TO SERVE
– 3 tsp coarsely ground peanuts
– 3 tsp uncooked and coarsely ground Thai rice

TO MAKE YOUR OWN NUOC CHAM SAUCE
– 1 tsp soft brown sugar
– 3 tsp rice vinegar
– 2 UK/US tbsp (1 ½ AU tbsp) tamari sauce
– 2 UK/US tbsp (1 ½ AU tbsp) water

Using a well-sharpened knife, cut the beef into small cubes and put them in a large mixing bowl. Cut the chilli peppers in half, rinse away the seeds and chop the peppers finely, wearing gloves, if you wish, to protect your hands. Finely chop the white bulbs of the onions and a couple of the green stems. Peel the ginger root and cut it into long, thin batons. Wash and dry the basil and coriander leaves, then chop or snip them. Finely slice the lemongrass stalks, using only the pale yellow section that is tender. Combine all of these prepared ingredients in the bowl, turning them for even distribution. Set this tartare aside briefly.

For the dressing, use a fine-bladed zester tool to scrape the zest from the 2 limes, reserving the zested limes for the garnish. Put the zest in a small mixing bowl. Add the olive oil and nuoc cham sauce and whisk until the mixture emulsifies.

If making your own nuoc cham sauce, dissolve the sugar in the rice vinegar and whisk in the tamari sauce. When smooth, gradually stir in the water to make a sauce.

Pour the dressing over the tartare mixture and stir to distribute flavours. Cover the bowl with cling film (plastic wrap) and chill the tartare in the refrigerator.

To complete and serve the tartare, arrange it on individual plates. Sprinkle over the coarsely ground peanuts and rice. Cut the reserved, zested, limes into quarters, and add a couple to each plate.

TARTARE OF BEEF AND VEAL WITH PARMESAN AND ROCKET

SERVES 4 – PREPARATION 20 MINUTES

– 300 g (11 oz) fillet or tenderloin of beef
– 300 g (11 oz) round of veal, from the upper-hind leg
– a small handful of rocket/arugula
– 4 halves of sun-dried tomatoes
– 50 g (2 oz) Parmesan
– 2 UK/US tbsp (1 ½ AU tbsp) crushed or coarsely ground pine nuts
– 4 UK/US tbsp (3 AU tbsp) olive oil
– sea salt and freshly ground pepper

- -

Wash and dry the rocket then chop it coarsely or snip it. Cut the halves of sun-dried tomatoes into small pieces. Put these ingredients into a large mixing bowl. Using a well-sharpened knife, cut the beef and veal into small cubes (see page 18), transferring them to the bowl as you work. Use a peeler, or small sharp knife, to scrape shavings from the Parmesan, letting them fall into the bowl. Add the pine nuts, then toss the mixture to distribute the ingredients evenly. To complete the tartare, drizzle over the olive oil, add a little salt and pepper and toss again.

Either serve the tartare immediately or cover it and keep it chilled in the refrigerator until you are ready. Whatever you do, don't wait until the next day!

TRADITIONAL & KNIFE-CUT STEAK TARTARE

SERVES 4 – PREPARATION 15 MINUTES

- 600 g (1 lb 5 oz) prime minced/ lean ground beef
- 3 sprigs of flat leaf parsley
- 3 sprigs of tarragon
- about 12 small chives
- 2-3 shallots, or 2 small mild-tasting onions
- 100 g (4 oz) capers
- Tabasco sauce (optional)

FOR THE SEASONING
- 4 UK/US tbsp (3 AU tbsp) olive oil
- 3 tsp mustard
- 1 tsp Worcestershire sauce

- 2 UK/US tbsp (1 ½ AU tbsp) tomato paste or ketchup
- salt and pepper

FOR THE ACCOMPANIMENT
- 4 eggs
- Tabasco sauce (optional)

In a mixing bowl large enough to accommodate the meat, make the seasoning for the tartare: whisk together vigorously the olive oil and mustard. When the mixture is smooth, whisk in the Worcestershire sauce and tomato paste or ketchup. Season to taste. Add the minced meat and toss it well to distribute the seasoning evenly; set aside briefly.

Wash and dry the parsley, tarragon and chives, then chop or snip them. Peel and finely chop the shallots. Drain the capers. Incorporate these ingredients into the tartare. If you like your tartare hot, add a little Tabasco. Cover the tartare with cling film (plastic wrap) and chill it until you are almost ready to serve.

Separate the egg yolks from the whites, slipping each yolk back into a half-egg-shell and arranging it on a plate to serve as an accompaniment for the tartare. If you like, add a small touch of salt and pepper to each yolk. Put the whites in a covered container and keep them for another recipe, such as meringues.

To serve, arrange the tartare on individual plates. Offer each guest an egg yolk, and accompaniments of ketchup, Tabasco and Worcestershire sauce. In this way, guests can adjust the seasoning of the tartare to suit their personal taste.

KNIFE-CUT VERSION
Replace the minced beef with 600 g (1 lb 5 oz) of sirloin or, better still, fillet or tenderloin. It is important to use a prime cut, so ask your favourite butcher for advice. Use a well-sharpened knife to cut the meat into thin strips and then into small dice (see page 18).

BEEF TARTARE WITH HERBS

SERVES 4 — PREPARATION 10 MINUTES

– 600 g (1 lb 5 oz) prime minced/lean ground beef
– 6 sprigs of flat leaf parsley
– 4 sprigs of basil
– 6 sprigs of coriander/cilantro
– 6 sprigs of chervil
– 4 sprigs of tarragon
– 2 sprigs of mint
– about 12 small chives
– 2 shallots
– 4 UK/US tbsp (3 AU tbsp) olive oil
– salt and pepper

- -

Wash and dry all the herbs. Pluck the leaves from their stems and either chop the leaves or snip them with scissors. Cut the chives to a length of your liking and set the herbs aside briefly. Peel and finely chop the shallots. In a mixing bowl, combine the olive oil with the meat and shallots. Add the herbs to the mixture, and toss the tartare to distribute the ingredients evenly. Add salt and pepper to taste. Cover the bowl with cling film (plastic wrap) and keep the tartare chilled until you are ready to serve it.

NOTE
I recommend that you make this tartare at the last moment.

Serve this tartare with a green salad to which you have added a few mildly piquant herbs such as chervil, marjoram or parsley.

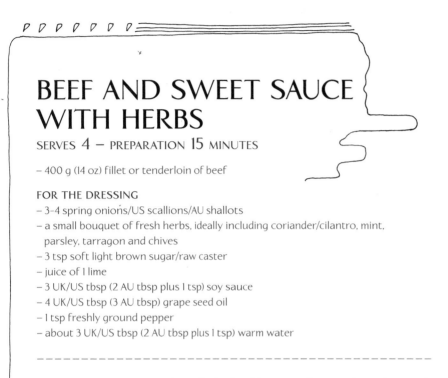

BEEF AND SWEET SAUCE WITH HERBS

SERVES 4 – PREPARATION 15 MINUTES

– 400 g (14 oz) fillet or tenderloin of beef

FOR THE DRESSING
– 3-4 spring onions/US scallions/AU shallots
– a small bouquet of fresh herbs, ideally including coriander/cilantro, mint,
  parsley, tarragon and chives
– 3 tsp soft light brown sugar/raw caster
– juice of 1 lime
– 3 UK/US tbsp (2 AU tbsp plus 1 tsp) soy sauce
– 4 UK/US tbsp (3 AU tbsp) grape seed oil
– 1 tsp freshly ground pepper
– about 3 UK/US tbsp (2 AU tbsp plus 1 tsp) warm water

Ask your butcher to cut through the beef horizontally to make 4 slices each weighing 100 g (4 oz).

Trim the onions and wash and dry the herbs; set these ingredients aside briefly. You can make the dressing by hand, or you can use a food processor or blender with a very gentle pulsing action. For the latter option, put the onions and herbs in the bowl of the machine. Add the remaining ingredients for the dressing except the water. Pulse the mixture very briefly so that the onion and herbs become chopped very coarsely rather than finely; they should retain their identity. Transfer the dressing to a small bowl. To make the dressing liquid enough to coat the meat, stir in just enough luke-warm water to achieve the right consistency.

Alternatively, chop the onions and herbs coarsely by hand. Mix together the sugar and lime juice, stir in the soy sauce and whisk in the oil and pepper. Stir in the chopped onions and herbs. Add enough luke-warm water to loosen the dressing to a desired coating consistency.

Serve each slice of meat coated in the dressing.

MARINATED ROUND OF VEAL

SERVES 4 – PREPARATION 15 MINUTES

MARINATING 4 HOURS

– 400 g (14 oz) round of veal, from upper-hind leg

FOR THE SAUCE
– 12 cherry tomatoes
– 12 bulbs and 4 stems of spring onions/US scallions/AU shallots
– 4 UK/US tbsp (3 AU tbsp) olive oil
– 2 UK/US tbsp (1 1/2 AU tbsp) capers
– a few leaves of basil
– 1 tsp Espelette pepper
– juice and zest of 1 lime
– fleur de sel and pepper

- -

Ask your butcher to cut the round of veal horizontally into four 100 g (3 1/2 oz) slices.

To make the marinade, first cut the cherry tomatoes in quarters and finely chop the spring onions (scallions). Arrange the slices of veal in a large shallow dish. Drizzle the olive oil on top of the meat. Then add the sliced tomatoes, chopped spring onions (scallions), capers, basil leaves, Espelette pepper and lime juice and zest. Cover the dish with cling film (plastic wrap) and place it in the refrigerator for 4 hours. Turn the slices of veal regularly so that the meat is evenly coated.

Remove the dish from the refrigerator and unwrap it. Add a little fleur de sel and pepper immediately before serving. Serve the marinated veal with a nice, crunchy green salad or sucrine lettuce hearts.

BARELY
****
COOKED

WHITE FISH WITH FENNEL AND CHORIZO

SERVES 4 – PREPARATION 20 MINUTES

COOKING 4 MINUTES

– 4 thick fillets weighing about 120 g (4 ½ oz) each of very fresh yellow Pollock,
  or very fresh coley, cod or whiting
– 1 red pepper
– 1 yellow pepper
– 1 fennel bulb
– ½ lemon confit
– 20 g (¾ oz) chorizo sausage
– olive oil
– a pinch of powdered saffron
– a few sprigs of flat leaf parsley (optional)
– fleur de sel and freshly ground pepper

Wash and pat dry the vegetables. Cut the peppers in half, scrape out the seeds
and then chop the flesh into dice. Chop the fennel into dice. Rinse and pat dry
the lemon confit then chop it into tiny dice. Chop the chorizo into tiny dice
of the same size. Put all these ingredients into a bowl and stir in about one
tablespoon of olive oil and a pinch of saffron. Wash, dry and chop the parsley if
you are including it; reserve it for the garnish.

Wash the fish and pat it dry. Heat a large frying pan (skillet) or an electric grill
plate, adding just enough olive oil to coat the base. When it is hot, add the fillets
of fish. Seal them in the heat on one side for 3 minutes then turn them over. Add
the mixture of peppers, fennel, lemon and chorizo. Continue to cook the fish for
a further minute or until it is cooked to your liking. Season lightly with salt. Add
freshly ground pepper and chopped parsley, if you wish.

NOTE

The electrical grill plate is a very popular appliance in France. Sometimes called
a table grill, it sits on the worktop and plugs in like any other kitchen appliance.
With both ribbed and smooth surfaces, it cooks at a very high temperature thus
locking in the flavour of the food. It can also be thermostatically controlled;
keeping food hot once it's cooked. If you have an electric grill plate, do not
hesitate to use it for this recipe.

SPICY TUNA STEAK

SERVES 6 – PREPARATION 10 MINUTES

COOKING 8 MINUTES

– 800 g (1 lb 12 oz) fillet of tuna
– olive oil
– 2 UK/US tbsp (1 ½ AU tbsp) soy sauce

FOR THE SPICE MIXTURE
– 1 tsp cumin seeds
– 2 tsp fennel seeds
– 2 tsp pink peppercorns
– 1 tsp black peppercorns
– 1 tsp coriander seeds
– 1 tsp powdered coriander
– 2 tsp powdered ginger

- -

Ask your fishmonger to prepare 6 very fresh tuna steaks of the same size. Wash the fish and pat it dry. Cover and reserve in the refrigerator until required.

Put all the ingredients for the spice mixture into the bowl of a grinder, food processor or blender with a grinder attachment. Pulse the ingredients in short bursts until the seeds and peppercorns are crushed coarsely, or crushed to the texture of your choice. You can also crush the seeds and peppercorns with a pestle and mortar or a coffee grinder - you can even put them in a tea towel and crush them with a hammer.

Spread out the crushed mixture on a large plate. Brush the tuna steaks on both sides with olive oil, then press both sides into the spice mixture to coat them.

Heat a large frying pan (skillet), or an electric grill plate, adding just enough olive oil to coat the base. When it is hot, add the tuna steaks. Cook them for 2 minutes on each side so that the tuna remains red on the inside yet forms a sealed crust of spice on the outside.

Transfer to serving plates. Drizzle each steak with a little soy sauce and serve with a good green salad.

NOTE
If you have an electric grill plate, do not hesitate to use it for this recipe.

WHITE FISH IN GREEN BROTH

SERVES 4 – PREPARATION 15 MINUTES

COOKING 20 MINUTES

– 300 g (11 oz) very fresh white fish, such as sea bream, yellow pollock,
  cod, coley or whiting

FOR THE BROTH
– leafy tops from a bunch of radish
– a handful of young spinach leaves
– 10 mint leaves
– 1 litre (4 1/4 US / 4 AU cups) water
– fleur de sel and freshly ground pepper

TO SERVE
– pumpkin seed oil
– 3 tsp poppy seeds

Wash the fish, pat it dry and then cut it into small cubes, as for a tartare (see page 16). Cover and set aside in the refrigerator.

Wash and dry the leaves of radish, spinach and mint. To make the broth, put the water in a saucepan and bring it to a boil. Add salt, pepper and the leaves of the radish and spinach. Adjust the heat to maintain a very gentle simmer for 20 minutes. Stir in the mint leaves and remove the broth from the heat. Using the blender of your choice, blend the broth just long enough to break down the leaves into coarsely chopped pieces. (If you are not going to serve the dish straight away, leave the broth to cool down then reheat and strain it at the last moment.)

Just before serving, have ready 4 serving bowls. Strain the hot broth through a fine sieve set over a large bowl, reserving the green mixture of leaves. Put a tablespoon of the leaf mixture in the bottom of each serving bowl. Add the fish, distributing it evenly. Ladle over the hot broth. Sprinkle with poppy seeds, salt and pepper. Drizzle with a fine stream of pumpkin seed oil and serve without delay.

THAI BROTH WITH BEEF

FOR 10 ROLLS – PREPARATION 25 MINUTES

CHILLING 1 HOUR

– 200 g (7 oz) fillet or tenderloin of beef
– 4 florets of cauliflower
– 1 carrot
– 1 baby turnip
– 1 uncooked small red beetroot/beet

FOR THE BROTH

– 800 ml (3 ¹/₃ US/3 ¹/₅ AU cups) water
– 1 peeled clove garlic
– 3 cm (1¹/₄ inches) fresh ginger root
– stems from 1 bunch of coriander/cilantro

– 1 small red chilli pepper
– 8 fresh or dried kaffir lime leaves
– 3 tsp soy sauce
– about 1 tbsp sesame oil

ACCOMPANIMENTS TO SERVE

– 1 lime, cut into quarters
– leaves from 1 bunch of coriander/cilantro

Wash and dry the vegetables and herbs. Cut the clove of garlic in half. Slice the ginger into thin strips. Chop the coriander stems coarsely and set the leaves aside for the garnish. Split the red chilli pepper in half – wearing gloves to protect your hands if you like – then scrape out the seeds; chop the flesh coarsely. To make the broth, put the water in a saucepan and bring it to the boil. Add all of the ingredients for the broth including the soy sauce and sesame oil. Adjust the heat to maintain a very gentle simmer for 30 minutes.

While the broth simmers, grate the florets of cauliflower so as to obtain semolina-like crumbs and a few paper-thin slices; set aside. Peel the carrot, turnip and the beetroot. Cut these vegetables into the smallest of dice; set aside. Cut the beef into small cubes.

When you are almost ready to serve, distribute the beef between 4 serving bowls. Arrange the reserved vegetables on top. Have ready 2 small bowls for the accompaniments of coriander and lime. Snip the reserved coriander leaves. Put the leaves in one bowl and the quarters of lime in the other.

Strain the broth through a fine sieve set over a fairly large serving bowl, discarding the solids. (If you are not going to serve the dish straight away, let the broth get cold, then reheat it at the last moment.) Offer each guest a bowl of the assembled beef and vegetables. Serve the broth separately at the table, ladling it over each assembly of beef. Let guests help themselves to the accompaniments of coriander and lime.

NOTE

Kaffir lime leaves, fresh and dried, are now more readily available in supermarkets as a result of the popularity of Thai cuisine. You can also source Kaffir lime leaves from many Asian grocers and, failing that, you will certainly find them online. You can also replace them with 4 stalks of lemongrass finely sliced into rounds.

QUICKLY ROASTED PUMPKIN WITH HONEY AND ORANGE

SERVES 4 — PREPARATION 15 MINUTES

COOKING 4 MINUTES

– about 500 g (1 lb 1 oz) orange-flesh squash or
  traditional pumpkin
– olive oil

FOR THE SAUCE
– juice and zest of 2 organic oranges
– 2 tsp liquid honey
– a pinch of powdered cumin
– fleur de sel and freshly ground pepper

_ _

Wash and dry the squash. With a sharp knife, cut it into slices 1-2 cm ($^3/_8$–$^3/_4$ inch) thick. You will need strong arms if you are using a traditional potiron pumpkin! Scrape away the seeds if you like, and any fibrous material from the slices.

To prepare the sauce, put the orange juice, honey, cumin and a little salt and pepper in a saucepan. Stir the ingredients together over low to medium heat until you achieve a smooth syrupy consistency. Remove from the heat and keep the sauce warm.

Heat a large frying pan (skillet) or an electric grill plate, adding just enough olive oil to coat the base. When it is hot, add the slices of squash. When the heat has sealed the flesh of the squash, after about 30 seconds, lower the heat and continue to cook the slices on one side for 4 $^1/_2$ minutes. Turn over the slices, lowering the heat again if necessary, and cook them for a further minute on the other side.

Serve the slices straight away, surrounded by the sauce.

VARIATION
For a version which cooks the squash to a greater degree, cut it into small cubes and proceed in the same way.

FILLET OF BEEF WITH ROCKET AND PARMESAN

SERVES 4 – PREPARATION 10 MINUTES

COOKING 4 MINUTES

– 500 g (1 lb 1 oz) fillet or tenderloin of beef
– 100 g (4 oz) rocket/arugula
– 25 g (1 oz) Parmesan cheese
– 3 UK/US tbsp (2 AU tbsp plus 1 tsp) olive oil
– fleur de sel and freshly ground pepper

_____

During the preparation of this dish, it is essential to heat 4 large serving plates, in a low 120°C (240°F, gas mark ½) oven.

Wash and dry the rocket and set it aside. Heat a large frying pan (skillet) or an electric grill plate, adding just enough olive oil to coat the base. When it is hot, add the fillet of beef in one piece and cook it over lively heat for 2 minutes on each side. Wrap the beef in aluminium foil and leave it to rest for at least 10 minutes in a warm place. Carve the beef into slices and arrange them on the warm serving plates. Garnish each helping with a few rocket leaves. Use a peeler or sharp knife to take shavings from the Parmesan and scatter them on top. Drizzle a thin stream of olive oil over the assembly. Season with salt and pepper and serve immediately.

TATAKI OF SALMON

SERVES 4 – PREPARATION 15 MINUTES

COOKING 4 MINUTES

MARINATING 2 HOURS

CHILLING 3 HOURS

– 400 g (14 oz) fillet of salmon cut from the back
  of the fish lengthways, in two pieces, to make 2
  thick fillets each weighing about 200 g (7 oz)
– 50 g (2 oz) sesame seeds
– 3 tsp neutral-flavoured oil, such as rapeseed,
  canola, sunflower or vegetable

FOR THE MARINADE

– ½ peeled clove garlic
– 50 g (2 oz) grated fresh ginger root
– 2 UK/US tbsp (1 ½ AU tbsp) nuoc cham sauce

——

To make the marinade for the fish, chop the garlic very finely and combine it with the grated ginger and nuoc cham. If making your own nuoc cham, see page 156.

Leaving the skin of the salmon in place, wash the 2 fillets and pat them dry. Remove any remaining bones with tweezers. Sit them in a shallow dish, snugly side by side. Pour over the marinade. Cover the dish with cling film (plastic wrap) and marinate the salmon in the refrigerator for 2 hours, turning the fillets occasionally.

Meanwhile, sautée the sesame seeds in a frying pan (skillet). Set the pan over medium heat for 1-2 minutes, shaking the pan and stirring to ensure the seeds cook evenly without burning. Set the seeds aside on a flat plate.

Drain the fish and wipe it dry. Heat a large frying pan (skillet), adding just enough olive oil to coat the base. When it is hot, add the 2 fillets of salmon and cook them for 30 seconds on each side. Remove the skin from the fish and press each fillet of salmon into the sesame seeds to make an even all-round coating. Wrap each fillet tightly in cling film. Chill the 2 pieces in the refrigerator for 3 hours.

Just before serving, carve each fillet of salmon into 4 long thin slices using a sharp knife. Arrange 2 slices on each plate and add a little of the sauce. Serve immediately.

VARIATION
You can replace the salmon with tuna.

NOTE
Tataki is a popular Japanese way of preparing fish as well as prime cuts of beef. To prepare tataki, the fish or meat is cut into thick pieces and marinated in rice vinegar or mirin. It is then seared in one piece, either over an open flame or in a frying pan, before being thinly sliced. Often it is served with soy sauce, shredded spring onions and grated ginger. Here it is offered with a delicious Vietnamese nuoc cham sauce.

RED MULLET WITH TOMATO CONFIT AND PARMESAN

SERVES 4 – PREPARATION 10 MINUTES

COOKING 5 MINUTES

– 16 scaled fillets of red mullet, skin in place
– 50 g (2 oz) tomato confit
– 1/2 bunch of basil leaves
– a few mint leaves
– olive oil

TO SERVE
– 25 g (1 oz) Parmesan
– fleur de sel and freshly ground pepper

————————————————————————

Chop the tomato confit coarsely. Wash and dry the herbs. Set these ingredients aside.

Wash the fish, pat it dry and then coat each fillet lightly in olive oil. Line the bottom of a large frying pan (skillet) or an electric grill plate with greaseproof or parchment paper. Heat the frying pan or grill plate. Cook the 16 fillets and their garnish of tomatoes and herbs in batches, or in two separate frying pans. Depending on the size of the pan, put about half or one-third of the quantity of fillets, skin-side down, in a single layer and sear them on one side only for 2-3 minutes. Add tomatoes and herbs in proportion and cook for a further 1-2 minutes. Repeat the process until all the fillets and their garnish have been cooked.

Have ready 4 warm serving plates. Transfer 4 fillets to each plate and distribute the garnish all around. Use a peeler or a small, sharp knife to take shavings from the Parmesan and scatter them on top. Sprinkle with salt and pepper and serve immediately.

HOT VARATION
If you have a hot and spicy palate, you can drizzle the finished dish with a little chilli oil at the last moment.

VEAL WITH VEGETABLES AND LIQUORICE

SERVES 4 – PREPARATION 20 MINUTES

COOKING 5 MINUTES

INFUSING 20 MINUTES

RESTING TIME FOR THE VEAL 10 MINUTES

– 200 g (7 oz) round of veal from the upper-hind leg
– 1 uncooked chestnut
– 100 g (4 oz) broad beans, removed from their pods and skins
– 100 g (4 oz) petits pois/French baby peas
– 2-3 spring onions/US scallions/AU shallots (optional)
– olive oil
– fleur de sel and freshly ground pepper

FOR THE BROTH
– 800 ml (3 ⅓ US/3 ⅕ AU cups) chicken stock
– 1 stick of liquorice

Over medium heat bring the chicken stock to a boil. Remove it from the heat. Grate the stick of liquorice on top of the stock and, when you have covered the surface, snap the liquorice in half and drop it into the stock. Cover the stock with a lid and leave it to infuse for 20 minutes.

Cut the veal into ½ cm (¼ inch) dice, as for a tartare cut by hand (see page 18). Distribute the veal between 4 serving bowls and add the peeled broad beans and baby peas.

Strain the infused broth. Reheat it and ladle it into the bowls. Season with a little salt and pepper then leave it to rest for 10 minutes.

Just before serving, remove the shell from the chestnut and use a very sharp knife to cut it into the thinnest of slices or strips. Add these to the broth along with thinly sliced spring onions if you are including them. Drizzle over a thin stream of olive oil and serve.

NOTE
I buy my sticks of liquorice from health-food stores. They are sometimes to be found in pharmacies and they are readily available online.

SCALLOP AND KOMBU BROTH

SERVES 4 – PREPARATION 15 MINUTES

COOKING 30 MINUTES

INFUSING 10 MINUTES

– 12 scallops, without the coral
– 100 g (4 oz) Japanese enoki mushrooms

FOR THE BROTH
– 800 ml (3 ⅓ US/3 ⅕ AU cups) water
– 20 g (¾ oz) kombu seaweed
– 20 g (¾ oz) dried bonito flakes
– 20 g (¾ oz) shiso leaves, preferably red

Rinse and pat dry the scallops, cover them and set aside in the refrigerator. If the bases of the enoki mushrooms are hard, trim them. Quickly rinse the mushrooms and drain them on paper towels; set aside. Rinse and pat dry the shiso leaves.

To make the broth, put the water in a saucepan and bring it to a boil. Add the kombu seaweed and immediately adjust the heat to maintain a very gentle simmer for 30 minutes. Strain the broth through a fine sieve set over a bowl and discard the kombu which will have given up its goodness. Add the dried bonito flakes to the strained liquid, cover it and leave it to infuse for 10 minutes. To complete the broth, strain it again and discard the bonito. If you are going to serve the dish straight away, keep the broth warm, otherwise let it cool and reheat it later.

To serve, have ready 4 wide serving bowls and put 3 whole scallops in each. Distribute the enoki mushrooms between the bowls. Ladle over the hot broth and add 5 shiso leaves to each bowl. Serve immediately.

NOTE
Apart from the scallops, I buy all the ingredients for this dish from a Japanese grocers or I order them online. Kombu seaweed (also known as Japanese kelp) is rich in iodine and has taken off particularly in the UK. Antonin Bonnet, Helen Darrroze, Heston Blumenthal and Richard Corrigan have all recently created stunning recipes with it. The kombu is not necessarily visible in the recipes because it is often strained out or used in a small quantity. Its claim to fame is not merely the high iodine content but also its ability to intensify the taste of the surrounding flavours with which it mingles.

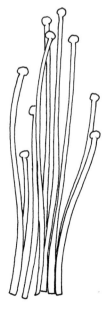

LITTLE GEMS
AND LITTLE SEEDS

SERVES 4 – PREPARATION 10 MINUTES

COOKING 3 MINUTES

– 4 hearts of little gem/baby cos lettuce, or regular cos/romaine lettuce
– 1 tsp pumpkin seeds
– 1 tsp sunflower seeds
– 1 tsp linseeds
– 2 UK/US tbsp (1 ½ AU tbsp) maple syrup
– olive oil
– salt and freshly ground pepper

_____

Crush the seeds coarsely: you can either do this by putting them in a grinder and pulsing very briefly, or you can crush them with a pestle and mortar or, failing that, wrap them in a tea-towel and crush them with a rolling pin. Set the crushed seeds aside briefly. Wash and dry the lettuces. Cut the hearts of lettuce in half. Brush them on the cut-side with olive oil.

Heat a large frying pan (skillet) or an electric grill plate, without adding any oil. When this is hot, add the hearts cut-side down and cook them on one side only for about 3 minutes.

Have ready 4 serving plates. Transfer 2 halved lettuce hearts to each plate and drizzle over a little maple syrup. Sprinkle with the mixed crushed seeds, salt and pepper. Serve without delay.

Note

If you are using the slightly larger regular or romaine lettuce, cut the hearts into third or quarters before grilling.

TOMATOES WITH LEMON CONFIT AND MINT

SERVES 4 – PREPARATION 10 MINUTES

COOKING 4 MINUTES

– 800 g (1 lb 12 oz) beef/beefsteak tomatoes
– 1 lemon confit (or about 8 slices)
– 2 sprigs of mint
– olive oil
– freshly ground pepper

Heat a large frying pan (skillet) or an electric grill plate. Meanwhile, rinse the lemon confit. If you are using a whole lemon, cut it into thin round slices, removing the pips. Wash and dry the tomatoes and mint leaves. If the mint leaves are small, keep them whole; snip larger ones. Cut the tomatoes into slices about 1.5 cm (½ inch) thick.

Brush all the slices of tomato and lemon confit with olive oil. Arrange them in a single layer on the hot grill plate and cook them for 2 minutes on each side.

Serve the cooked tomatoes and lemon immediately, seasoned with freshly ground pepper, mint leaves and, if you like, a little salt.

ROASTED VEGETABLES WITH BOTTARGA

SERVES 4 – PREPARATION 20 MINUTES
COOKING 1 MINUTE

– 1 small and firm yellow courgette/zucchini or squash
– 2 purple carrots
– 2 orange carrots
– 4 asparagus spears
– 2 fat-bulbed new onions with green stems
– 1 small yellow turnip
– olive oil
– 20 g (³/₄ oz) bottarga/dried salted grey mullet roe
– freshly ground pepper

Wash all the vegetables thoroughly, taking extra care if they are not organic. Peel them all except for the courgettes. Using a mandoline or a very sharp knife, cut the courgettes, carrots, asparagus spears and onions into long thin slices. Cut the turnips into slices of a similar thickness. Transfer the vegetables to a large mixing bowl. Drizzle over olive oil and toss the vegetables to coat them evenly; set aside. Cut half of the bottarga lengthways into long thin slices; set the slices aside until the last moment. Grate the remaining half.

Heat a large dry frying pan (skillet) and, when it is very hot, add the vegetables and cook them on one side for one minute. Season them with freshly ground pepper and sprinkle with the grated bottarga. Turn the vegetables over, count 10 seconds, and then remove them from the heat. Serve the vegetables immediately, interspersed with the reserved slices of bottarga.

NOTE

Bottarga is a Mediterranean delicacy of salted, cured fish roe, typically from grey mullet, tuna and – to a lesser extent – swordfish. The grey mullet variety, Bottarga di Muggine, is the most highly acclaimed and its price reflects this. Usually it comes from Sardinia. It is often available in good Italian delicatessens but, failing that, is available vacuum-sealed and frozen.

Since I adore bottarga, I suggest you offer even more of it to those who would like to indulge.

CUTTLEFISH WITH CHORIZO AND TARRAGON

SERVES 4 – PREPARATION 10 MINUTES

CHILLING 1 HOUR

COOKING 4 MINUTES

– 500 g (1 lb 1 oz) small, cleaned and prepared cuttlefish, squid or calamari
– 50 g (2 oz) chorizo sausage
– 2 hearts of little gem/baby cos or romaine
– 4 sprigs of tarragon
– 2 UK/US tbsp (1 ½ AU tbsp) olive oil
– salt and freshly ground pepper

Wash and dry the lettuces and sprigs of tarragon. Wash and pat dry the cuttlefish. Cut the hearts of lettuce into quarters or halves depending on size. Transfer the pieces of lettuce to a large shallow dish. Add the cuttlefish and sprigs of tarragon. Drizzle over the olive oil and turn the ingredients to coat them evenly. Season with salt and pepper. Cover with cling film (plastic wrap) and marinate the cuttlefish mixture in the refrigerator for at least 1 hour.

Towards the end of the marinating period, cut the chorizo sausage into small to medium-sized dice.

Remove the marinated cuttlefish mixture from the refrigerator. Heat a very large sauteuse or deep-sided frying pan (skillet). When it is very hot, add the cuttlefish and the pieces of lettuce cut-side down, reserving the tarragon. Cook the ingredients for 2 minutes. Add the chorizo, distributing it evenly and stirring the bottom of the pan with a wooden spoon. Turn the ingredients and leave them to cook for a further 2 minutes. Chop or snip the reserved tarragon leaves. Distribute the cuttlefish and lettuces to 4 serving plates. Sprinkle with the tarragon leaves and serve straight away.

VARIATION

If you wish, you can substitute cuttlefish for squid or calamari. All are closely related cephalopod molluscs. Cuttlefish differ slightly from squid and calamari in having a small inner 'cuttlebone'. There are many species of each and, when they are not available fresh, can often be bought clean and frozen.

NOTE

If you have an electric grill plate, do not hesitate to get it out for this recipe – you'll give your friends a real treat!

VEAL STEAK
WITH MUSHROOMS

SERVES 4 – PREPARATION 20 MINUTES

COOKING 10 MINUTES

RESTING 30 MINUTES

– 500 g (1 lb 1 oz) fillet or tenderloin of veal, cut into 4 thick slices
– 15g (½ oz) melted butter
– 1 small bunch of purslane or mâche/lamb's lettuce or alternative
  leaves such as spinach or rocket
– 200g (7 oz) seasonal mushrooms, choosing from chanterelles,
  oyster, shiitake, porcini, chestnut
– olive oil
– sea salt and freshly ground pepper

Brush each slice of veal with melted butter and season it with freshly ground pepper. Heat a large frying pan (skillet) or an electric grill plate. When it reaches a high heat, add the slices of veal and sear them for 2 minutes on each side, basting regularly with the pan juices. Transfer the seared veal to a wooden cutting board. Cover it with aluminium foil and leave the veal to rest for 30 minutes.

Wash and dry the purslane. To prepare the mushrooms, clean the stems free of soil and trim away tough ends. Wipe the mushroom caps with a damp cloth. If the mushrooms are small and of an even size, leave them whole; otherwise, cut the mushrooms in halves or quarters in a way that retains an attractive shape.

About 5 minutes before serving the dish, reheat the frying pan or electric grill plate. Add a drizzle of olive oil along with the mushrooms and cook them over a lively heat for 3 minutes without stirring. Add the veal to the mushrooms and cook for 1 more minute. Sprinkle with sea salt and freshly ground pepper.

To serve, distribute the mushrooms amongst 4 serving plates. Add a little purslane and place a piece of veal on top. Serve straight away.

LANGOUSTINES, VANILLA AND YELLOW SQUASH

SERVES 4 – PREPARATION 25 MINUTES

MARINATING 1 HOUR – COOKING 2 MINUTES

– 8 large or 12 smaller langoustines/Dublin bay
  prawns/jumbo shrimp
– 2 small yellow courgette/zucchini
– 4 large asparagus spears
– 2 sprigs of basil, leaves separated
– olive oil
– salt and freshly ground pepper

FOR THE MARINADE
– 100 ml (3/8 US / 2/5 AU cup) olive oil
– 1 vanilla pod/bean

To flavour the oil for the marinade, measure the olive oil into a medium-sized bowl. With a small, sharp knife split the vanilla pod in half lengthways and scrape out the vanilla seeds into the oil. Stir to mix and then set aside briefly.

To prepare the langoustine, pull off the head and legs and then peel away the shell. With a small, sharp knife make a shallow slit down the centre of the curved back of each langoustine and, if there is a black intestinal vein, remove it with the point of the knife – it tastes very bitter. Rinse the langoustines under cold running water and dry gently with kitchen paper. Add the langoustines to the vanilla-scented oil and toss gently. Cover the bowl with cling film (plastic wrap) and chill in the refrigerator for at least 1 hour.

Wash the vegetables well, leaving the skin of the courgettes intact. Rinse and pat dry the basil. Cut the first courgette into small dice. Cut the second courgette in half lengthways, then in half again lengthways, to obtain 4 long sticks. Peel away any tough fibres from the asparagus spears then cut them in half lengthways. Cut each half into thirds to make small sticks. Transfer the vegetables to a bowl. Drizzle them with olive oil and mix to coat them evenly. Drain the langoustines, reserving the vanilla oil.

Have ready 4 serving plates. Distribute the diced courgette amongst the plates and drizzle with the reserved oil. Heat two large dry frying pans (skillets) over high heat. Add the langoustines to the first frying pan and add the long sticks of courgette along with the short sticks of asparagus to the second frying pan. Drizzle these vegetables with a little olive oil and add salt and freshly ground pepper. Cook the langoustines and the vegetables for a good minute over high heat. Turn over the langoustines and vegetables and cook for a further 30 seconds. Transfer the cooked vegetables to the serving plates and arrange the langoustines on top. Garnish with the basil leaves and serve immediately.

HOME-MADE BASICS

SESAME AND CLEMENTINE DRESSING (100% RAW)

SERVES 4 – PREPARATION 5 MINUTES

– 2 tsp tahini
– juice of 2 clementines or tangerines
– about 1 cm (³/₈ inch) grated fresh ginger root
– 2 tsp maple syrup
– 1 tsp organic soy sauce
– 3 tsp rice vinegar
– 1 tsp sunflower oil
– freshly ground pepper

Put all the ingredients, except for the pepper, into the bowl of a food processor or blender and blend them to obtain a smooth mixture. Add freshly ground pepper to taste.

Serve this vinaigrette with salads of grated carrots, radishes or turnips – or simply with any crunchy salad that will be complemented by the dressing's sweet, spicy edge.

NOTE

Tahini is a thick purée or paste made from ground sesame seeds. You can find it in most supermarkets and health-food stores. It is usually sold in jars.

SUNDRIED TOMATO VINAIGRETTE (100% RAW)

FOR 1 SMALL JAR (2 OR 3 SALADS) – PREPARATION 5 MINUTES

– 6 halves of sun-dried tomatoes
– 2 UK/US tbsp (1 ½ AU tbsp) pine nuts
– 5 UK/US tbsp (3 AU tbsp plus 3 tsp) balsamic vinegar
– 1 small tsp sea salt
– 200 ml (⅞ US cup / ⅘ AU cup) olive oil
– 3 tsp freshly ground pepper

_ _

Put all the ingredients into the bowl of a food processor or blender and pulse the mixture a few times to obtain a slightly creamy vinaigrette that retains some small morsels of tomato and pine nuts.

You can store this vinaigrette in a jar in the refrigerator.

I like making this vinaigrette to dress salads which include wafer-thin slices of vegetables that I have usually cut with a mandoline. Generally speaking the vinaigrette goes well with salads, green or otherwise, which have a touch of 'crunch' about them.

VINAIGRETTE WITH AVOCADO, ORANGE AND SOY (100% RAW)

SERVES 6 – PREPARATION 5 MINUTES

– flesh of 1 ripe avocado
– juice of ½ orange
– 3 tsp soy sauce
– 2 UK/US tbsp (1 ½ AU tbsp) rice vinegar
– 1 ½ - 2 tsp homemade tartare of seaweed (see page 220)
– sea salt and freshly ground pepper
– 50 ml (about ⅕ US/⅕ AU cup) olive oil

Put all of the ingredients, except for the olive oil, into the bowl of a food processor and blend to a smooth mixture which retains a few tiny morsels of seaweed. Incorporate the oil in stages, gradually creating an emulsified vinaigrette. If the vinaigrette is a little too thick for your liking, stir in a little more oil.

Serve this lively flavoured vinaigrette with a salad of tender young spinach leaves and beetroot.

VARIATION
You can replace the tartare of seaweed with grated ginger root.

BRAZILIAN VINAIGRETTE (100% RAW)

FOR 1 SMALL JAR (3 OR 4 SALADS) – PREPARATION 5 MINUTES

– 120 ml (½ US/AU cup) olive oil
– 3 UK/US tbsp (2 AU tbsp plus 1 tsp) fresh orange juice
– 2 tsp fresh lemon juice
– 1 tsp honey
– 2 tsp red wine vinegar
– about ½ tsp finely chopped small red chilli pepper (hot variety)
  or Cayenne pepper
– salt and pepper

Whisk together all of the ingredients to obtain a full-bodied vinaigrette with flecks of red chilli pepper.

There is a little salad that I love serving with this hot, fruity vinaigrette. For 4 people, I cut a small pineapple into dice and cut the flesh of 2 avocados into small pieces. I then mix these elements with a good handful or so of crisp salad leaves and some other crunchy salad items if I have them to hand. I toss the salad and, at the last moment, add the Brazilian Vinaigrette along with the chopped leaves of about half a bunch of coriander/cilantro.

MILD AND FRUITY GUACAMOLE (100% RAW)

SERVES 4-6 — PREPARATION 10 MINUTES

- – 2 just ripe avocados
- – 2-3 washed and chopped
  sorrel leaves
- – about 3 spring onions/US
  scallions/AU shallots
- – juice of 1/2 orange
- – a pinch of Espelette pepper
- – 1/2 tsp sea salt

Wash the spring onions and chop them coarsely. Just before you are ready to blend the ingredients, peel the avocados and reserve one of their stones. Put all of the ingredients into the bowl of a food processor or blender. Pulse the mixture briefly then check that the taste and texture is to your liking. Adjust seasoning, adding more salt and Espelette pepper as required. For a smoother texture, blend again.

If, on the other hand, you like a chunky texture, make the guacamole in a slightly different way: mash the avocados with a fork and set aside. Blend the remaining ingredients in a machine and then combine this mixture with the mashed avocados, stirring the two elements together by hand.

TIP

If you don't intend to serve the guacamole straight away, sit the reserved stone in the mixture to prevent it from turning brown. As an added precaution during a long waiting period, cover the entire guacamole and stone with cling film (plastic wrap) and place it in the refrigerator until you are ready to serve.

HOT AND SPICY GUACAMOLE (100% RAW)

SERVES 4-6 — PREPARATION 10 MINUTES

- 2 ripe avocados
- about 4 spring onions/US scallions/AU shallots
- 1/2 – 1 washed, deseeded and finely chopped small red chilli pepper
- 1 peeled, cored and deseeded tomato
- 3 sprigs of washed and chopped coriander/cilantro
- juice of 1 lime
- 4-5 drops Tabasco sauce
- 1/2 tsp sea salt

Wash the spring onions and chop one of them into rough shapes for the garnish; set this aside. Chop the remaining onions coarsely. Just before you are ready to blend the ingredients, peel the avocados and reserve one of their stones. Put all of the ingredients into the bowl of a food processor or blender. Pulse the mixture briefly and then check that the taste and texture is to your liking. You can adjust seasoning and add more chilli pepper and Tabasco for a hotter, spicier taste. For a smoother texture, blend again.

If, on the other hand, you like a chunky texture, make the guacamole in a slightly different way: mash the avocados with a fork and set aside. Blend the remaining ingredients in a machine and then combine this mixture with the mashed avocados, stirring the two elements together by hand.

Serve in a bowl with the garnish of onion on top.

AVOCADO MAYONNAISE (100% RAW)

SERVES 6 — PREPARATION 5 MINUTES

– the flesh of 2 avocados
– ⅓ bunch of chives
– 100 ml (³/₈ US/²/₅ AU cup) olive oil
– 2 UK/US tbsp (1 ½ AU tbsp) maple syrup
– juice of 1 very juicy lime (or the juice of 2 firmer limes)
– Tabasco sauce a few drops
– salt and freshly ground pepper

_____

Wash the chives and chop them coarsely. Just before you are ready to blend the ingredients, peel the avocados and reserve one of their stones. Put all of the ingredients into the bowl of a food processor or blender. Blend them to a smooth purée which retains a few small flecks of chives.

If you are going to serve the sauce more or less straight away, transfer it to a pretty serving bowl. If you like you can sit the reserved stone in it to ensure that the sauce does not turn brown. Alternatively, keep the sauce in a sealed jar.

VARIATION
You can replace the chives with other fresh herbs, such as coriander (cilantro), chervil or basil. You can also substitute tarragon but, if you do, use less of it to compensate for its exceptionally assertive flavour.

Whereas with real mayonnaise, the oil is combined with egg yolks, here it is combined with avocado. I adore this recipe, which doubles as a dip and a sauce. As a dip, I serve it with crudities and raw sliced vegetables of all kinds. This makes a good appetizer to serve with an aperitif. As a sauce, this fake mayo makes an excellent companion for raw beef marinated in pepper (see page 147).

PETITS POIS DIP WITH TAHINI ⓘ 100% RAW

FOR 1 SMALL JAR — PREPARATION 15 MINUTES

– 100g (4 oz/ ²/₃ US/AU cup) petits pois/French baby peas
– 30 g (1 oz/ 1/6 US/AU cup) tahini
– ¹/₂ peeled shallot/AU eschallot
– 50 ml (¹/₅ AU cup) olive oil
– ¹/₂ tsp ground nutmeg
– 1 tsp soy sauce
– salt and pepper

- -

Put all of the ingredients into the bowl of a food processor or blender and pulse the mixture a few times to obtain a dip with a fairly smooth consistency. Taste and adjust seasoning.

Transfer to a decorative bowl for serving. If you are not going to use the dip immediately, cover it with cling film (plastic wrap) and keep it in the refrigerator until you are ready. The dip is delicious accompanied by raw seasonal vegetables.

NOTE
Tahini is a thick purée, or paste, made from ground sesame seeds. You can find it in most supermarkets and health-food stores. It is usually sold in jars.

TARAMA HOUSE-STYLE

SERVES 6-8 – PREPARATION 15 MINUTES

– 300 g (11 oz) fresh smoked cod's roe
– 2 UK/US tbsp (1 ½ AU tbsp) sunflower oil
– juice of ½ - 1 lemon
– 2 – 4 tbsp crème fraiche or Greek yogurt
– freshly ground pepper

- -

Carefully peel away the membrane from the sac of smoked cod's roe and use a blunt knife to help scrape the sections of roe into a large mixing bowl. With a fork, mash the sections of roe until you achieve a homogenous paste. Little by little, stir in the oil to smooth and loosen the mixture. (Should there be any clumps of roe remaining, you can pulse them briefly using a blender but, generally speaking, a tarama made by hand is better.)

Gradually incorporate the lemon juice and the yoghurt, tasting every so often and adding as much or as little of these ingredients as suits your personal taste. Season with freshly ground pepper. Cover and chill the tarama until you are ready to use it. Serve it with wedges of lemon. As an accompaniment, offer fine slices of black radish, white Chinese Daikon radish or even cucumber.

NOTE
You can usually obtain smoked cod's roe from your fishmonger, but you may have to order it in advance. It is well worth the effort.

This taramasalata is nothing like the commercial versions that you may have tasted.

A SIDE ORDER
OF SEAWEED (100% RAW)

FOR 1 SMALL JAR — PREPARATION 10 MINUTES

SOAKING/REHYDRATING 15 MINUTES

MARINATING 2 HOURS

– a good handful of mixed dried seaweed (from a selection
  of wakame, dulse, nori, kombu)
– 1 shallot
– 3 tsp capers
– 1 organic lemon
– 6 UK/US tbsp (4 1/2 AU tbsp) olive oil

Soak the seaweed in water for 15 minutes to rehydrate it. Drain it and, if the seaweed is in large pieces, chop it (or blend it for a few seconds but taking care not to reduce it to a purée). Transfer the seaweed to a mixing bowl and set it aside briefly.

Peel the shallot and chop it finely. Chop the capers finely. Stir these ingredients into the seaweed. Using a fine zesting tool, scrape pith-free zest from the lemon. Cut the zested lemon in half. Squeeze juice from one half, stirring it into the seaweed mixture; reserve the remaining half. Stir in the olive oil. Taste and add more lemon juice if desired.

Transfer the tartare of seaweed to a jar, seal it and put it in the refrigerator. Leave it to marinate for 2 hours before serving it. The tartare will keep in the refrigerator for several days.

Serve this tangy tartare of seaweed with raw vegetables as an appetizer with an aperitif. Alternatively, offer it as an accompaniment for tartare of veal (or another raw meat and fish dish of your choice).

SWEET

TART CRUST 1 (100% RAW)

SERVES 8-10 – PREPARATION 10 MINUTES

SOAKING 1 HOUR

FREEZING 1 HOUR

– 170 g (6 oz / 1 ⅛ US/AU cup)
  blanched whole almonds
– 50 g (2 oz / ⅓ US/AU cup)
  pine nuts
– 13 pitted dates
– 3 tbsp (2 AU tbsp plus 1 tsp)
  honey
– about 1-2 tbsp water

To make the dough, begin by soaking the almonds in a small amount of warm water for at least 1 hour. Drain them and blend them with the pine nuts, dates, honey and enough water to obtain a reasonably smooth mixture. It does not matter if some small morsels remain — it will actually be better that way! The dough should be very well mixed and should not stick to your fingers. If it is too dry, then the dates are probably not moist enough, so add a little more water very gradually.

You can store the dough, either wrapped in cling film (plastic wrap) or placed inside an airtight container, in the refrigerator for a few days or until needed.

To line the tart mould, use your fingers to spread out the dough in the bottom of the mould to a thickness of 1 cm (³/₈ inch). With the flat, damp base of a glass, pack the dough down well into the edges.

Before you fill the tart, place the lined mould in the freezer for 1 hour or in the refrigerator for several hours.

TART CRUST 2 (100% RAW)

SERVES **8-10** — PREPARATION **10** MINUTES

SOAKING **1** HOUR

FREEZING **1** HOUR

- 170 g (6 oz / 1 1/8 US/AU cups)
  blanched whole almonds
- 170 g (6 oz / 1 1/3 US/AU cups)
  shelled walnuts
- 10 pitted dates
- about 50 ml (1/4 US/1/5 AU
  cup) water

To make the dough, begin by soaking the almonds in a small amount of warm water for at least 1 hour. Drain them and blend them with the walnuts, dates and enough water to obtain a reasonably smooth mixture. It does not matter if some small morsels remain — it will actually be better that way! The dough should be very well mixed and should not stick to your fingers. If it is too dry, then the dates are probably not moist enough, so add a little more water very gradually.

You can store the dough, either wrapped in cling film (plastic wrap) or placed inside an airtight container, in the refrigerator for a few days or until needed.

To line the tart mould, use your fingers to spread out the dough in the bottom of the mould to a thickness of 1 cm (3/8 inch). With the flat, damp base of a glass, pack the dough down well into the edges.

Before you fill the tart, place it in the freezer for 1 hour or in the refrigerator for several hours.

ALMOND MILK (100% RAW)

FOR 1 LITRE – PREPARATION 30 MINUTES
SOAKING 8-12 HOURS

‑‑‑

– 150 g (5 oz / 1 US/AU cup)
  whole almonds in their skin
– about 240-250 ml (1 US/AU
  cup) mineral or filtered water
  for soaking the almonds
– 1 litre (4 1/4 US/4 AU cups)
  mineral (or filtered) water

Soak the almonds in mineral water for 8-12 hours. Rinse and drain the almonds, then peel away their skins, which should come off very easily. Make sure that all the almonds are perfectly clean.

Blend the almonds with the litre of mineral water in four 15-second pulses. Be sure to wait 30 seconds between pulses so that the almonds do not overheat, which would make them lose their nutritional value. Pass the mixture through a nylon sieve; do not use a metal one, or the milk will take on a metallic flavour.

. . . . . CHILLED AND SWEET

For a chilled version that is sweetened with fruit, blend the almond milk with 10 very fresh dates, pitted and chopped, and some ice cubes. If the resulting mixture is not smooth enough for your liking, you can sieve it or blend it a little more. Drink it straight away or put it in the freezer for an hour and enjoy it ice-cold… either way, it's marvellous.

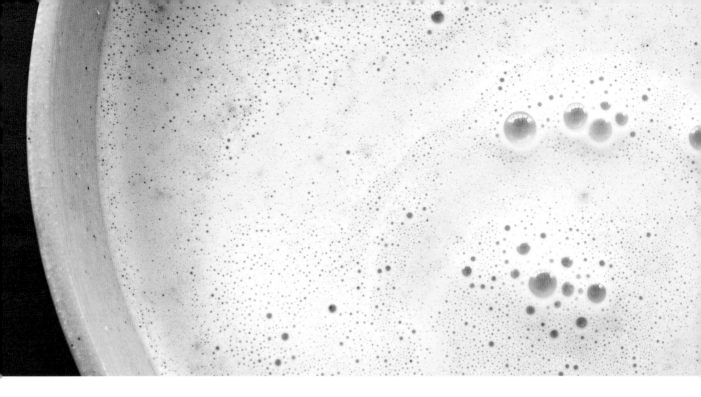

HAZELNUT MILK (100% RAW)

FOR 1 LITRE — PREPARATION 10 MINUTES
SOAKING 8-12 HOURS

- 150 g (5 oz / 1 US/AU cup)
  blanched whole hazelnuts
- about 240-250 ml (1 US/AU
  cup) mineral or filtered water
  for soaking the hazelnuts
- 1 litre (4 1/4 US/4 AU cups)
  mineral or filtered water

Soak the hazelnuts in mineral water for 8-12 hours. Rinse and drain the hazelnuts, and make sure that they are all perfectly clean.

Blend the hazelnuts with the litre of mineral water in four 15-second pulses. Be sure to wait 30 seconds between pulses, so that the hazelnuts do not overheat, which would make them lose their nutritional value. Pass the mixture through a nylon sieve; do not use a metal one, or the milk will take on a metallic flavour.

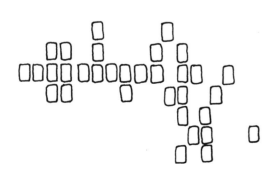

. . . CHOCOLATE-FLAVOURED 100% RAW

For a chocolaty version, blend the hazelnut milk with 4 very fresh dates, pitted and chopped, and 5 UK/US tablespoons (3 AU tablespoons plus 3 teaspoons) of organic cocoa powder or carob powder, which can be found in health-food stores. Enjoy it immediately, or refrigerate it and save it for breakfast.

You can incorporate this chocolate-flavoured hazelnut milk into smoothies or serve it with desserts, but it is also delicious just by itself!

CASHEW NUT AND CHOCOLATE SPREAD (100% RAW)

FOR 1 SMALL JAR – PREPARATION 5 MINUTES

– 6 UK/US tbsp (4 ½ AU tbsp) cashew nut purée/cashew butter
– 2 UK/US tbsp (1 ½ AU tbsp) organic cocoa powder
– 2 UK/US tbsp (1 ½ AU tbsp) agave syrup/nectar
– 3 tbsp (2 AU tbsp plus 1 tsp) organic icing sugar/confectioner's sugar
– 3 tsp ground hazelnuts

Blend the ingredients until smooth, either using a machine or mixing by hand. Transfer the blended spread to an airtight jar.

VARIATION

You can replace the cashew nut purée with hazelnut purée (butter), in which case you should omit the ground hazelnuts. You should be able to find both nut purées at your favourite health-food store. If not, you can order them online.

This spread is ideal for filling pastry cases or pie shells or for spreading onto crispbreads, crackers and muffins. You can also blend 1 tablespoon with a large glass of almond or hazelnut milk. . . yummy!

CHOCOLATE-COCONUT TART (100% RAW)

SERVES 8 – PREPARATION 20 MINUTES

FREEZING 1 HOUR

SOAKING 5 HOURS

CHILLING 2 HOURS

FOR THE TART CRUST
– 170 g (6 oz /1 1/8 US/AU cup) blanched whole almonds
– 170 g (6 oz /1 1/3 US/AU cup) shelled walnuts
– 10 pitted dates
– about 50 ml (1/4 US/1/5 AU cup) water
– 1 tsp sea salt

FOR THE FILLING
– 150 g (5 oz / 1 US/AU cup) cashew nuts/cashews
– mineral or filtered water for soaking the cashew nuts
– 35 g (1 1/4 oz / 1/3 US/AU cup) organic cocoa powder
– 25 g (about 1/4 US/AU cup) grated fresh coconut flesh
– 100 ml (3/8 US/2/5 AU cup) agave syrup/nectar
– 4 tbsp (3 AU tbsp) coconut butter
– 1 tsp sea salt

Soak the cashew nuts for the filling in mineral water for at least 5 hours or overnight if possible.

To make the pastry case for the tart, follow the instructions for Tart Crust 2 (see page 225), adding a teaspoon of sea salt to the mixture before blending.

Use the palms of your hands to spread out the dough in a tart tin with a removable base. With the flat, damp base of a glass, continue to press the dough into the tin. Remove any excess dough from around the edges. Let the pastry case rest in the freezer for 1 hour.

For the filling, drain the cashew nuts and blend them with the cocoa powder, coconut flesh, agave syrup, coconut butter and sea salt. Remove the pastry case from the freezer and pour the filling into the shell. Refrigerate the tart for at least 2 hours before serving.

STRABWERRY-SICHUAN TARTLETS (100% RAW)

SERVES 6 – PREPARATION 20 MINUTES

FREEZING 1 HOUR

FOR THE INDIVIDUAL TARTLET CASES
– 170 g (6 oz /1 1/8 US/AU cups) blanched
  whole almonds
– 50 g (2 oz / 1/3 US/AU cup) pine nuts
– 13 pitted dates
– 3 tbsp (2 AU tbsp plus 1 tsp) honey
– about 1-2 tbsp water
– 1 tsp sea salt

FOR THE TOPPING
– 500 g (1 lb 1 oz / 3 1/3 US/AU cups) Gariguette
  or other seasonal strawberries
– ground Sichuan/Szechuan pepper to taste

EQUIPMENT
– pastry cutter or saucer about 9 cm (3.5 inches)
  in diameter

_____

To make the tartlet cases, follow the instructions for Tart Crust 1 (see page 224), adding a teaspoon of sea salt to the mixture before blending.

Spread out the dough by hand onto a large work surface. With the flat, damp base of a glass, pack the dough down well. Use a pastry cutter or small saucer to cut out 6 rounds. Wrap each one in greaseproof or parchment paper and let them rest in the freezer for 1 hour or in the refrigerator for several hours.

Quickly wash the strawberries and drain them. Hull the berries and cut each one into 3 or 4 teardrop-shaped slices. Remove the rounds of dough from the freezer or refrigerator and unwrap them. Place the rounds on individual dessert plates or on a serving platter. To assemble the tartlets, arrange the strawberries in a rosette on each round base. Keep the tartlets refrigerated until ready to serve, but do not wait too long, or the berries will spoil!

Just before serving, add a little freshly ground Sichuan pepper on top of the tartlets.

You may have some dough left over, which you can freeze and use for another recipe.

RAW MINI CAKES WITH HERBS

SERVES 6 – PREPARATION 15 MINUTES

FREEZING 1 HOUR

SOAKING 1 HOUR

CHILLING 1 HOUR 30 MINUTES

FOR THE INDIVIDUAL CAKE BASES
– 170 g (6 oz /1 1/8 US/AU cup) blanched whole almonds
– 50 g (2 oz /1/3 US/AU cup) pine nuts
– 13 pitted dates
– 3 tbsp (2 AU tbsp plus 1 tsp) honey
– about 1-2 tbsp water
– 1 tsp sea salt
– 3 tsp lemon juice

FOR THE WHIPPED HERB-CREAM FILLING
– 150 g (5 oz /7/8 US/AU cup) cashew nuts/cashews
– 200 ml (7/8 US/4/5 AU cup) almond milk (see page 226)
– 50 ml (1/4 US/Đ AU cup) liquid honey
– 1/2 tsp salt
– 3 tsp lecithin
– 1/2 sprig of chopped chervil
– 1/2 bunch of chopped chives
– salt and pepper of your choice

EQUIPMENT
– 9 cm (3.5 inches) in diameter smooth-edged pastry cutter or food ring

---

To make the individual bases for the cakes, follow the instructions for Tart Crust 1 (see page 224), adding a teaspoon of sea salt and 3 teaspoons of lemon juice to the mixture before blending. Spread out the dough by hand, and use a pastry cutter to cut out 6 rounds of dough. Wrap each one in greaseproof or parchment paper and let them rest in the freezer for 1 hour or in the refrigerator for several hours.

For the filling, soak the cashew nuts in mineral water for 1 hour. Drain them and then blend them with the almond milk, honey and salt, to obtain a smooth mixture. Add the lecithin and chopped herbs to the mixture and season with salt and pepper to taste. Place the mixture in the refrigerator for 1 hour.

Remove the 6 rounds of dough from the freezer or refrigerator and unwrap them. Arrange them on individual dessert plates or on a serving platter. Assemble the cakes one by one: place the pastry cutter around each base and fill the circle with one-sixth of the whipped herb-cream. Remove the pastry cutter carefully, wash it and repeat the procedure for each cake. Refrigerate the mini cakes for at least 30 minutes.

VARIATION
For a sweet version, replace the herbs with soft red fruit and arrange it on the bases before adding the whipped cream topping without the salt and pepper.

NOTE
Lecithin can be found in health-food stores.

LEMON TART (100% RAW)

SERVES 8-10 – PREPARATION 20 MINUTES

FREEZING 1 HOUR

SOAKING 5 HOURS

CHILLING 2 HOURS

FOR THE TART CRUST
– 170 g (6 oz / 1 1/8 US/AU cup) blanched whole
– 50 g (2 oz / 1/3 US/AU cup) pine nuts
– 13 pitted dates
– 3 tbsp (2 AU tbsp plus 1 tsp) honey
– about 1-2 tbsp water
– zest of 2 organic lemons

FOR THE FILLING
– 150 g (5 oz / 1 US/AU cup) cashew nuts/cashews
– 1 tsp pure vanilla powder
– lemon juice taken from the 2 lemons above
– 4 tbsp (3 AU tbsp) coconut oil

—————————————————————————————————————

Soak the cashew nuts in mineral water for at least 5 hours or overnight if possible.

To make the pastry case for the tart, first remove the zest from both lemons using a fine zester tool to scrape away tiny pith-free shreds. Reserve the zested lemons for the lemon juice for the filling. Follow the instructions for Tart Crust 1 (see page 224), adding half of the zest to the mixture before blending and reserving the remaining zest for a final garnish.

Use the palms of your hands to spread out the dough in a tart tin with a removable base. With the flat, damp base of a glass, continue to press the dough into the tin. Remove any excess dough from around the edges. Let the pastry case rest in the freezer for 1 hour.

For the filling, drain the cashew nuts and blend them in a food processor or blender with the vanilla powder, lemon juice and coconut oil, to obtain a smooth mixture. Pour the mixture into the pastry case, and refrigerate the tart for at least 2 hours.

Immediately before serving, garnish the tart with the remaining lemon zest scattered on top.

NOTE
Pure vanilla powder can be found online, or you can make it at home by grinding vanilla pods (beans) in a coffee grinder. You can buy coconut oil in health-food stores and online.

MANGO, PASSION FRUIT AND MASCARPONE ICE CREAM

SERVES 6 – PREPARATION 15 MINUTES

– 4 passion fruits
– 450 g (1 lb / 2 ½ US/AU cups) frozen mango flesh
– 125 g (4 ½ oz / 1 US/AU cup) mascarpone
– 3 tsp tightly packed soft brown sugar

_____

Cut each passion fruit in half, and scoop out the fruit. Pass the fruit through a nylon sieve to retrieve the juice but not the seeds. Put the frozen mango, passion fruit juice, mascarpone and sugar in the bowl of a food processor or blender and blend the ingredients to a soft ice cream consistency, which retains a few morsels of fruit. The size of the morsels and exact consistency will depend on personal taste. Serve immediately.

VARIATION

The ice cream is at its best when freshly-made. If you do not want to eat it straight away, you can store it in an airtight container in the freezer until later, though it won't be as creamy!

NOTE

Peel the mangoes, cut the flesh into chunks and then freeze the flesh for at least 3 hours before making the ice cream.

PINEAPPLE, SAGE AND GINGER SORBET (100% RAW)

SERVES 4 – PREPARATION 10 MINUTES

– 1 kg (2.2 lb / 5 ½ US/AU cups) pineapple flesh cut into chunks and frozen
– about 2 cm (¾ inch) grated fresh ginger root
– 3-6 tsp maple syrup depending on the sweetness of the pineapple
– 5 torn sage leaves
– 2-3 turns of the peppermill freshly ground pepper

Put the frozen pineapple chunks, grated ginger root and maple syrup in the bowl of a food processor and blend the ingredients to a reasonably homogenous mixture. Next, change the blade of the food processor for one that is ordinarily used for kneading dough, add the sage and pepper, and then blend the mixture again briefly to achieve a soft, smooth-grained sorbet. Serve immediately.

The sorbet is at its best when freshly-made. If you do not want to eat it straight away, you can store it in an airtight container in the freezer. It will remain good for about 3 hours. However, the longer you freeze it, the less smooth it becomes. Remove it from the freezer 15 minutes before serving.

VARIATION

If you would like to make this sorbet with fresh pineapple, remove the pineapple's skin and eyes. Cut the flesh into chunks, discarding the hard core, and freeze the pineapple flesh for at least 3 hours before making the sorbet. If the pineapple is very sweet, add a minimal amount of maple syrup. You can also replace the sage with basil.

ORANGE AND
BLUEBERRY SORBET (100% RAW)

SERVES 6 – PREPARATION 10 MINUTES

– 5 oranges
– 250 g (8 ½ oz/2 ½ US/AU cups) frozen blueberries
– about 2 cm (³/₄ inch) grated fresh ginger root
– juice of 1 lemon

_ _

Peel the oranges closely, taking away all the white pith. Working over a small
bowl, use a small, sharp knife to cut down each side of each section of membrane,
letting the freed orange segments fall into the bowl. Catch the juice and discard
the membrane. Put the orange flesh in a freezer bag or container and freeze it
for several hours or until firm.

Put the frozen orange flesh, frozen blueberries, ginger and lemon juice into the
bowl of a food processor and blend the ingredients to a reasonably homogenous
mixture. To obtain a smoother-textured sorbet, change the blade of the food
processor for one that is usually used for kneading dough, and blend the
mixture again briefly to achieve a soft, smooth-grained sorbet with a few flecks
of blueberry. Arrange the sorbet on individual serving plates garnished, if you
like, with a few fresh whole blueberries. Serve immediately.

If you do not want to eat the sorbet straight away, you can store it in an airtight
container in the freezer. It will remain good for about 3 hours. However, the
longer you freeze it, the less smooth it becomes. Remove it from the freezer 15
minutes before serving.

STRAWBERRIES WITH WHIPPED HERB CREAM

SERVES 4 – PREPARATION 15 MINUTES

– 500 g (1 lb 1 oz / 3 1/3 US/AU cups) strawberries
– 250 ml (1 1/8 US/AU cups) cold whipping cream
– vanilla pod/bean
– 3 tsp cream of white balsamic vinegar
– 2 sprigs of mint

– 2 sprigs of tarragon
– 4 sprigs of chervil
– 1 organic lime
– ground Sichuan /Szechuan pepper to taste

Quickly wash the strawberries under a thin stream of luke-warm water. Drain them, hull them and cut them in half; set aside in a cool place, but not the refrigerator. Wash the herbs and pat them dry.

Pour the cream into a mixing bowl. Split the vanilla pod in half and use a knife to scrape out the seeds. Stir the vanilla seeds into the cream and set this vanilla-scented cream aside briefly. To make the whipped herb cream, you need to extract juice from the herbs and combine it with the cream of white balsamic vinegar and the vanilla-scented cream, all in a whipped form. There are various ways to do this, depending on the equipment to hand. If you have a gourmet cream whipper, choose option B:

A) Use a masticating juicer to extract juice from the herbs or, alternatively, use a regular bowl-type blender or food processor to blend the herbs to a pulp, then transform the pulp into juice by passing it through a fine sieve set over a bowl. Rub the pulp with the back of a wooden spoon to help squeeze out the juice. Set the juice aside. Use an electric beater to whip the reserved vanilla-scented cream, gradually incorporating the herb juice and the cream of white balsamic vinegar. Place the herb-flavoured cream in the refrigerator until you are ready to serve.

B) Use the blender of your choice to blend the vanilla-scented cream with the herbs. Pass this mixture through a sieve set over a bowl. Stir together the sieved herb cream and the cream of balsamic vinegar. Pour the combined mixture into a gourmet cream whipper, following manufacturer's instructions for charging and shaking it. Keep the whipper in the refrigerator until you are ready to serve

To serve, remove the whipped herb cream from the refrigerator. Arrange the strawberries on individual plates. Use a zester tool to scrape tiny zests from the lime and sprinkle them over the strawberries. Arrange a portion of whipped cream on each plate and add a little Sichuan pepper. Serve straight away.

PEARS, BEETROOT JUICE AND FETA

SERVES 6 – PREPARATION 20 MINUTES

– 3 ripe pears
– juice of 1/2 lemon
– 15 cubes of crumbled feta

FOR THE BEETROOT JUICE
– 1 uncooked beetroot
– 1 vanilla pod/bean
– 3 tsp maple syrup

Peel the pears, cut them into quarters and core them. Arrange the quarters on a plate in a single layer and sprinkle with the lemon juice. Cover the plate with cling film (plastic wrap) and set it aside in the refrigerator.

Chop or slice the beetroot coarsely and pass it through a centrifugal juicer to extract the juice; transfer the juice to a mixing bowl. Split the vanilla pod in half and use a knife to scrape out the seeds. Stir the vanilla seeds and maple syrup into the beetroot juice.

To serve, divide the beetroot juice between 6 plates and arrange 2 pear quarters in the middle of each pool of juice. Sprinkle the crumbled feta on top.

RECIPE INDEX

INDEX BY INGREDIENT

THANK YOU

Annie the raw foodist, thank you for your attentive re-reading of my recipes, your sound advice and your willingness to help without fuss.

My star guests, Thomas, Maud, Kaori, Alexandre, Samuel and James: thank you for having come on board and for having each created a recipe specially for this book. Thank you, too, for your availability and your kindness to everyone concerned.

The dazzling team: Emmanuel, Rose-Marie and Pauline, thank you for having allowed me to look into raw food in detail, for putting your trust in me and for making such beautiful books happen. To Rose-Marie, a special word of thanks for the long hours we both spent behind your computer screen… stress aside, it was a real pleasure

A particular thank you to my two treasures, Elodie and David, my fellow travellers, my tasters… it was my good fortune to put together a book which involved you and your talents. You sweated blood! Bravo!

To Jane, a special thank you for the lovely illustrations… and to Stanislas, a note of thanks for the 'moss' effect on the original French cover.

A tender thank you to Guillaume, Mae, Java and Joseph, whom I love very much.

ADDRESS BOOK:

LA MACHINE À COUDES
35 rue Nationale 92100 Boulogne – www.lamachineacoudes.com

EPICERIE GENERALE
43 rue de Verneuil 75007 Paris – www.epiceriegenerale.fr

NANASHI
57 rue Charlot 75003 --
31 rue de Paradis 75010 Paris -- www.nanashi.fr

TERROIRS D'AVENIR
7 rue du Nil 75002 Paris

BONES
43 rue Godefroy Cavaignac 75011 Paris

Frances Lincoln Limited
74–77 White Lion Street
London N1 9PF
www.franceslincoln.com

Raw Food French Style
Copyright © Frances Lincoln Limited 2014
Translation by Alexandra Carlier

Original Edition *CRU*
Copyright © Hachette-Livre (Marabout) 2013
Illustrations © Jane Teasdale
Photographs © Shutterstock, pages 24, 96, 162, 186, 232, 236, 238,
© Gettyimages / Kieran Scott p80 / James Worrell p84 / David Henderson
p88 / Stephen Shepherd p100 / Dwight Eschliman p106 / Joshua McCullough
p120 / Dana Menussi p172 / Mint Images/ Paul Edmondson p194 / Florence
Barreau p198 / Buena Vista Images p216

A catalogue record for this book is available from the British Library.

ISBN 9-780-7112-3542-7

Printed and bound in China

1 2 3 4 5 6 7 8 9